kiss my bundt

kiss my bundt

chrysta wilson

illustrated by kersti frigell

photographed by margeaux bestard

life of reiley

Dedication

To my mom, Melva,
and her sisters, Aunt Dia and Aunt Eleanor,
who always encouraged me to follow my dreams
no matter how crazy they seemed.

First printing 2009
ISBN: 978-0-9774120-2-0

art direction, design and production: Deborah Daly
editor: Amy Reiley
creative editor: Ronie Reiley
copy editor: Mark Siagh
illustrations: Kersti Frigell
photography: Margeaux Bestard
photo stylist: Courtney Cady
models: Courtney Cady, Seth Casriel, Mindy Richter, Montie Richter, Rose Rossi, and Vik Seshadri
test kitchen assistants: Larissa Buch, Delahna Flagg, Anne Janzen, Jessica Rabbiner, and Kendra Schussel
home cake testers: Nicole Bestard, Amy Concannon, Chris Cool, Megan Cooperman, Monica X. Delgado, Dan Fredman, Sarah Weber Gallo, Arlene Goss, Sarah Goss, Arthur Greenwald, Ngoc Hoang, Susie Jones, Alma Marquez, Kellee Mendoza, Marie Mercier, Rich Pedine, Lisa Peju, David Reiley, Jill Sazama, Patricia Simon, Tammy Sussman, and Arlene Winnick

PRINTED IN THE UNITED STATES OF AMERICA

contents

kiss my bundt

Introduction

As a child, I was a baking machine. I can remember begging my mom for an Easy Bake oven for my eighth birthday. When I got that oven, I was unstoppable. I began baking and selling cakes and treats in my front yard to all the neighborhood kids. My mother called me "Chrysta Iacocca," after the famous auto executive. A proper Southern woman from an early age, I baked and baked throughout my early teens and even entered my share of Girl Scout bake-offs.

When I was about 16, my mom and I moved from Florida to Danville, California, and for some reason, I stopped baking almost entirely. It wasn't until I was in graduate school at the University of Southern California that I started baking again, but this time my motivation was a little different. I was working as a community organizer and part of my job was getting people together to discuss and create plans on how we could collectively fix various issues. Bundt became my tool for bringing people together.

You see, calling a community meeting is not always enough to lure participants. But I quickly learned that if you bake, *they will come*... and if you create a comfortable environment, they will stay. So, I took the opportunity to create menus and experiment with new bundt cake flavors, intent on sufficiently wowing my colleagues. (This was a little trick of Southern hospitality I learned from my mother and her two sisters: Aunt Eleanor and Aunt Dia. I learned about cooking comfort foods from my mom and Aunt Eleanor, but Aunt Dia was the baker in the family. From her, I learned about the power of bundt. Her cakes would make peoples' eyes light up. They would be the center of any gathering or party. Dia's cake could draw people together. And I intended to use my bundts to do the same.)

A Boutique Bakery Is Born

My renewed interest in baking got me back in touch with Aunt Dia, with whom I was not as close since leaving the South. We would exchange recipes and she would ship bundt cakes to me in Los Angeles all the way from her hometown of Fayetteville, North Carolina. Eventually, I got calls from acquaintances asking if they could buy my creatively-flavored bundts. That's what first made me consider doing this baking thing as a business. At the time, I had just received a Master's degree in Public Administration, just finished a total of six years of intensive public policy training and had my dream job as Community Manager of a nonprofit. I thought (as did everyone in my family), "*How could I quit everything and start a bakery?*"

This decision weighed on my heart for about a year. I loved baking. People loved my cakes. I loved creating new flavors and people loved eating them. As I kept plugging away at my baking hobby, I inadvertently developed clients. Suddenly, my hobby was something more. It was a small business.

One Saturday in June of 2005–June 18th to be exact—I showed up at my real job but all I could think about was bundt cake and how I'd love to have a little pink and brown bakeshop that would be a gathering place for the community. I knew it would be a sassy little place and, of course, we'd serve bundts. As I continued to fantasize, I thought about what this little place would be called. Like a sack of bricks, it hit me. *Kiss My Bundt Bakery*. I called my Aunt Dia as soon as I left work and told her I wanted to open Kiss My Bundt.

Before I finish the story of how this little bakeshop came to be, I have to share one of the other questions I'm always asked by customers, "where did you learn to bake this?"

I was not a classically-trained baker. I learned the secrets of made-from-scratch baking by shadowing Aunt Dia during my childhood summers. She was a master. Everything she baked was amazing: red velvet, coconut, assorted varieties of pound cake—all of it excellent. I used to watch her take flour, sugar and eggs and make magic.

So when I called Aunt Dia with the idea of opening Kiss My Bundt, she was excited and incredibly encouraging. I think she always wanted to open her own small business. A few weeks later, my Aunt died of cancer.

But Aunt Dia's enthusiasm had me moving full steam ahead. I created a website to promote the business and began testing recipes. Before I knew it, I was running Kiss My Bundt Bakery as a web-based catering company. Even though I was building a clientele and growing the business, I continued to do it in my free time before and after my real work.

My mom thought it was crazy—but she was used to me and my crazy ideas. In the bakery's early days, she truly became Kiss My Bundt's biggest supporter. But a year after my Aunt Dia's death, my mother lost her own battle with cancer and passed away. It made me realize that life really is too short to put your dreams on hold.

With orders stacking up and with my client base mounting, I started looking for a location to open Kiss My Bundt Bakery. My storefront was secured on Thanksgiving 2007. The bakery was constructed and opened in August 2008.

What a journey! In less than four years, Kiss My Bundt Bakery has become a community bakery known for 100% made-from-scratch bundt cakes in creative, yet comforting flavors. In 2009, I launched a Baking Academy, where students are able to learn how to make cakes and confections from scratch and use them as tools to bring people together.

What Is a Bundt?

This is one of the regular questions asked by visitors to the bakery.

For someone like me, who grew up in the South where bundt cakes are everywhere, bundt is almost a way of life. Even as a child, I always thought bundt cakes

were far superior to any other shape of cake. They have the fluted edges and the fun and functional hole in the middle that helps this tall cake produce its signature moist, dense texture. And bundts are famously moist.

My first bundt pan was a beautiful, old, copper thing. It was my mother's. She got it some time in the late '70s, and she never used it. My mother wasn't a baker. When I moved away to college, I begged my mom for that pan. She didn't want to part with it—at first. She didn't use it but she didn't want to let it go. After begging and pleading, the Bundt pan was mine, and my future in baking bundts was set.

Why Bundt?

I remember being told as a kid that bundt is a "self-decorating cake." It took me years to realize what that meant. Glazes drizzled over the cake really accentuate its fluted edges and ridges. This cake doesn't need flowers, fondant or colored frostings for flair. Bundt is perfect as is. It's like a woman with all the right curves.

It is the perfect shape, with its cone up the center, for producing a moist, evenly-baked cake. And bundt makes a wonderful canvas for inventing new flavors. Once you get the technique down, you'll start to see how easy it is to change a cake with a different frosting or glaze. And you'll learn how easy it is to swap around an ingredient or two in the way I did to create this book and the menu for my bakeshop. You will fall in love with new flavors, and you'll fall in love with bundt.

· 1 ·

Tips in Plain English From a Veteran Baker

I love research. I want to know the ins and outs of a subject, ingredient, recipe. But when I started baking professionally, I couldn't find the information I wanted. The average cookbook gave me a method, not a reason or, if it offered a thorough explanation, the jargon was way too technical. Through trial and error—and by this, I mean some terrible, terrible cakes—I learned the hard way about the ingredients, methods and tools essential to making outstanding bundts. Part of my goal with this book is to provide home bakers with those kinds of tips, the ones that will help a regular person, like me, understand that baking from scratch is easy, affordable, all natural and, simply put, makes superior cakes.

Ingredients

Softened, Unsalted Butter
Baking is all about precision. Bakers must control all ingredients that go into their batter. There is no way to

know exactly how much salt is in regular, salted butter. This is why I use unsalted butter (and then add a specific amount of salt to the recipe). Doing so will give you a better cake. And it will definitely give you superior buttercream frosting.

In the bakery, I start the vanilla and pound cake batters with butter warmed to room temperature (this takes about 30 minutes in your average kitchen). If you haven't planned ahead and allowed your butter to warm before you begin making your batter, you will probably need to beat it for an extra 1–2 minutes to get the proper consistency.

Large Eggs at Room Temperature

Use large eggs for all the recipes in this book. Eggs MUST be warmed to room temperature in order to achieve the ideal cake consistency. As eggs warm up, they begin to expand. Expanded eggs add more volume and lightness to your cake batter than do eggs straight from the fridge. Warm eggs on a counter for 30 minutes or submerge in lukewarm water for 10 minutes before using.

Milk (never skim)

I recommend using whole milk for the recipes in this book because it gives more fat and volume to the cake. However, you could use a 2% or even 1% milk and reduce the fat of your cakes without much impact to the final cake. As with eggs, I recommend using milk at room temperature—although the temperature is not as critical with milk as it is with the eggs.

Using All-Purpose Flour

My recipes were formulated using all-purpose, rather than cake flour. (Cake flour die-hards will tell you that all-purpose flour can make a dense or tough cake. That can be true. But the basic difference between all-purpose and cake flour is that all-purpose has about 2% more gluten—the protein in flour that is released when a mixture of flour and liquid is agitated—than does cake flour. And for that 2% difference, stores charge a whole lot more money for cake flour.) I've learned that a couple tricks can give you soft, beautifully-textured cakes without shelling out the extra cash. First, sift the flour to break it up a little before adding it to the batter. Then, make sure you don't over mix your batter once you've added flour. Stop mixing your completed batter just after the last bit of flour has been incorporated, not a moment later. If you follow these tips, the glutens will not overdevelop.

Extracts (vanilla and beyond)

As a kid, my mom—who was not a baker—used imitation extracts in her baking to add a lot of flavor without fuss. At the bakery, I use pure extracts, like pure vanilla or pure orange extract. I use these ingredients to boost flavors of cakes in ways that artificial ingredients simply cannot. However, because purchasing multiple natural extracts can get expensive, I've noted on the recipes some places in which the flavor-boosting extracts are optional. You can also replace citrus extracts with extra zest, which I find gives a fairly similar intensity. I recommend using 1 tablespoon of zest for every teaspoon of extract in a recipe.

tips from a veteran baker

Bittersweet Chocolate and High-Fat Cocoa Powder

As all serious chocoholics know, you should never skimp on quality when using chocolate in a recipe. For chocolate ganache and glaze, I use bittersweet chocolate (60%-70% chocolate mass).

I do not use chocolate in cake batters because I find it makes the cake heavy and dry. For cakes, I use an unsweetened, Dutch-processed cocoa powder that has a high percent of cocoa butter (22%-24%). I find that this natural fat makes chocolate cakes extra rich and moist. You can use any cocoa powder with my recipes and the cake will come out fine, but once you go high fat, you'll never go back.

The Scraping Song

When the bakery first opened, I was noticing that sometimes the staff's batters had lumps of butter and sugar. One of my staff called them "butter blasters" because when the cake bakes, these lumps of butter and sugar melt and blast through the texture of the cake, leaving a gummy hole. "Butter blasters" come from failing to scrape the sides of the bowl while you're creaming butter and sugar.

The use of a rubber spatula is invaluable in creating smooth, uniform batters. To combat the "blasters," I wrote a song that I—probably to my staff's great annoyance—sang to remind everyone to scrape the mixing bowl. The key lyric was "scrape, scrape, scrape. Scraping is cool." Corny, perhaps, but the song worked!

Incorporating Air
(creaming and sifting)

Introducing air into your batter helps to give cake its light "crumb" or texture. Several of the steps in my recipes have been designed to incorporate the optimal amount of air into the batter.

Mixing (or creaming) the butter and sugar does more than mix the two ingredients. Creaming causes granulated sugar to rub up against the butter and create air bubbles. During baking, your leavening agents, baking soda or powder finish the job by expanding those bubbles, forcing the cake to rise.

Another step designed to ensure a light batter is sifting. By sifting, you loosen up the flour, making for easier incorporation into the batter. The less you mix the flour, the less of the flour's glutens are released and the fewer the glutens, the lighter the cake. In any instruction in this book calling for sifting, measure first, then sift.

Size Matters
(the mini, baby and big ol' bundt)

The recipes in this book are simply reliable cake recipes, meaning you can make my cakes in any shape of cake pan you wish, such as cupcakes or rounds. But I think my recipes turn out best in the bundt-shaped pan. I make three sizes of bundts at my bakery: the mini or "bundt cupcake", the baby bundt or "bundt muffin" and the 10-12 cup big ol' bundt." The cakes are referred to by these nicknames throughout the book.

Time and Temperature

All ovens are not created equal. And they are certainly not all treated equally. As a woman who has never known the joy of a new oven, I've learned the hard way how to gauge different ovens. This book calls for the cakes to be baked at 350 degrees Fahrenheit. But in one apartment, I had to bake them at 325 degrees and in another they wouldn't cook at anything less than 375 degrees. Ovens should be—and almost never are—recalibrated throughout their lives. Your oven may be a few degrees, or possibly many degrees, off. To combat irregularity, invest in an oven thermometer.

In this book, I recommend baking times, but your oven's temperature can drastically change the baking time. An oven thermometer will help you gauge baking time based on your oven's quirks. You may find that your oven's temperature is unsteady (this sometimes happens with gas ovens). In this case, you will want to frequently check your thermometer and your cake for doneness.

One last recommendation for targeting the perfect time and temperature is to check the cake 20 minutes before it should be done. If, at this point, the cake is already brown on top but raw in the middle, it is cooking too quickly. Reduce the heat a little, then continue to bake.

*See page 146 for recommended baking times.

A Question of Cooling

Inverting a bundt can be a frustrating step. (Liberal use of baking spray before you add batter to the pan really helps!) When you remove your finished cake from the oven, let it sit in the pan(s) for about 2 minutes. This allows the cake to pull away from the bottom and sides of the pan as it releases heat. Then, invert the cake onto a cooling rack or a plate to get it out of the pan. Cake pans, especially dark pans, retain heat and will continue cooking your cake even out of the oven. This is why I don't let my cakes sit in their pans for very long. If the cake doesn't release when inverted, let it sit in the pan for 15 minutes, then try again. Keep repeating this step until your cake comes out of the pan. And if—heaven forbid—the cake tears when it comes out of the pan, you can do a patch job by taking a little frosting or glaze to stick the torn pieces back on the cake. If a lot of the cake tears, patch it up and cover the cake with buttercream or cream cheese frosting—no one will ever know!

Tools of the Trade

There are a few tools that have become essential to my cake baking-business. You don't have to own them all—especially if you're just starting out. But trust me, you will immediately see results from the investment in these ten simple tools.

1. Stand Mixer

I use a stand mixer because it helps guarantee the development of the cake batter with the proper incorporation of air (this is essential for moist, fluffy cakes)— and it allows me the freedom to multitask in the kitchen. You can use an electric hand mixer (or mix by hand if you posses the bicep of a personal trainer). But after creaming butter with a hand mixer for a few months, especially with more dense batters like the Cinnamon Pecan Coffee Cake, you realize that a stand mixer is an excellent investment.

2. Rubber Spatula

This is one of the most essential tools I use in my bakery and one of the least expensive!

(See *The Scraping Song* earlier in this chapter.)

3. Measuring Cups, Spoons and Mixing Bowls

Measuring spoons, not regular household spoons, should be used for teaspoon [tsp] or tablespoon [tbsp] measures. You should have a set of measuring cups for dry ingredients and a liquid measure with a lip designed for pouring for wet ingredients. Invest in a few durable mixing bowls for those tasks that require a separate bowl. I find measuring ingredients before starting the batter gives me perfect accuracy.

4. Sifter

Powdered sugar, cocoa and flour often acquire clumps in storage. And clumps are the enemy of smooth batter. I like to use a sifter with a crank or a fine-mesh sieve or strainer for sifting. Do NOT purchase a sifter with a trigger. By your fifth cake you'll darn near have carpal tunnel. I learned this the hard way. When recipes in this book call for sifting, ingredients should be measured first, then sifted.

kiss my bundt

5. Microplane Zester

I used to use one of those pyramid-shaped things to zest my limes and lemons. I never really got a lot of zest, even though I grated the heck out of that citrus (and my hand)! A Microplane, (a long, stick-shaped grater based on a carpenter's rasp), is a wonderful invention because it easily removes the zest, (the colored rind of citrus fruits), without getting the bitter pith, (the white stuff beneath the rind).

6. Whisk

For sauces, frostings or even melting chocolate, you'll find the whisk can stir and incorporate your ingredients smoothly in ways a wooden spoon simply cannot.

7. Baking Spray with Flour

When I was a little girl, I learned all about greasing and flouring my bundt pan. I would rub butter around in the pan, then add a few tablespoons of flour and shake it around, tapping out the excess. This was to ensure that the cake would easily release from the pan. But modern science has propelled us into a world where we no longer need to grease and flour. Now you can buy a non-stick cooking spray with the flour already added. Spray your pan liberally with this marvel before adding your batter. When your cake is flipped from the pan, it will slide out with ease—without any of the chalky, flour coating that sometimes developed from old school greasing and flouring.

8. Bundt Pans

As your bundt experimentation grows, you may want to start a collection of pans in all 3 sizes. But the most essential is the big ol' (10 or 12 cup) bundt pan. Buy a light colored pan if you can find one—I have found that darker pans retain more heat and can burn the cake even if you follow baking times and frequently test for doneness. In my Baking Academy, at least one person per class will ask me about silicone bundt pans. When these pans first appeared, I wanted to love them. The concept of easy cake removal and easy cleanup makes sense to me. However, in my experience, silicone bundt pans do not produce the wonderful cakes I've come to expect from my metal pans. The cakes often brown on the outside before the middle cooks and the bake times can often be 50% more than the recipe recommends. Maybe I'm just old fashioned but metal, fluted pans are the only pans for me.

9. Cake Tester

You cannot reliably know a cake's doneness without testing. On a recent trip to a bakery supply store, I saw a cake tester that, when inserted into the cake, would turn blue if the cake is done. This is amazing technology. But I think a toothpick, popsicle stick, coffee stirrer or even a knife works fine. You'll know that the cake is done when the inserted tester comes out clean, free of batter or crumbs.

10. Cooling Rack

I like to flip my cooked bundts onto a wire cooling rack. The rack helps air circulate around the cakes. I do this at the bakery to drop the temperature and frost the cakes as soon as I can. You can cool your cakes on a plate but sometimes the sweat from the cake against the plate can make the bottom of the cake gummy.

• 2 •

Vanilla-Based Bundts

I call my vanilla cake the "blank canvas." This bundt is simply the kind of basic vanilla (or yellow) cake recipe I believe everyone should have in their baking repertoire. But I think of it as much more than vanilla cake. For me, it is a canvas and flavorful ingredients are swatches of color I can use to build my next masterpiece.

The way I make a new flavor of cake is perhaps not as thrilling as watching Van Gogh at work, however it is equally creative. I work from a theory that you can change one or both of two elements in the basic vanilla recipe to entirely alter the flavor of a cake. I refer to them as the liquid and the flavoring agent. This book is filled with the variations I've splashed across my canvas, but I've also built the book with the idea that every reader should, after practicing with a few of my cakes, have the confidence to create their own art.

For example, the liquid in the vanilla cake is 1 1/4 cups of milk. But the *kind* of liquid isn't as important as the *volume* of liquid. You could substitute some of the milk in this recipe for rum or coffee and wind up with a flavor entirely different from vanilla. You just need to keep the total amount of this liquid at 1 1/4 cups. As a general rule of thumb, I recommend that milk compose at least 1/2 cup of the liquid. In this chapter, I use a variety of liquids including wine, eggnog, fruit puree, coconut milk and Irish Cream.

The choice of liquid usually makes a fairly subtle change to the recipe but you can really make an impact by changing the flavoring agent. By flavoring agent I refer to the vanilla extract that flavors the vanilla cake along with other natural extracts, spices, fruits, etc. that add dimension to a basic yellow cake. I use a wide variety of flavoring agents in this chapter including ginger, citrus zest, instant coffee, fresh fruit, pudding mix, cinnamon and even basil.

vanilla-based bundts 27

Basic Vanilla Birthday Cake
"the blank canvas"

1. Preheat oven to 350 degrees.
2. Sift flour and baking powder and salt together. Set aside.
3. Beat butter with an electric mixer at medium speed until creamy, about 2 minutes.
4. Slowly add the sugar. Beat on medium speed until the mixture is fluffy, about 2 minutes.
5. Crack eggs into a separate bowl and add to batter one at a time. Then beat on medium speed for an additional 2 minutes.
6. Add vanilla to milk.
7. Beginning and ending with the flour, mix 1/3 of the flour into the wet mixture at a low speed, then 1/2 of the milk, alternating until all ingredients are mixed.
8. Transfer batter to cake pan(s) that have been coated with a baker's cooking spray that includes flour (or greased and floured), filling until cavity is about 3/4 full.
9. Bake cake(s) until an inserted toothpick or cake tester comes out clean—about 40 minutes for a big ol' bundt.

ingredients:

2 1/2 C flour
2 1/2 tsp baking powder
1/2 tsp salt
3/4 C unsalted butter
1 3/4 C sugar
3 eggs, room temperature
1 1/2 tsp vanilla
1 1/4 C whole milk

kiss my bundt

10. Invert cake(s) onto a cooling rack or serving plate. If cake resists, cool in the pan for 15 minutes before inverting. (If cake still resists, cool an additional 15 minutes in the pan.) Cool completely before frosting, at least 1 hour for a big ol' bundt.

Chrysta's Favorite Frostings & Finishing Touches:
Vanilla Buttercream, page 127
Chocolate Buttercream, page 127
Straw-Raz Buttercream, page 134
White Chocolate Curls
Colored Sugar Sprinkles

Cappuccino Cake

I created this cake to recapture the magic of a cappuccino I once sipped at a café in Venice's Piazza San Marco. This variation on vanilla cake is a perfect example of just how easy it is to completely change the flavor of vanilla batter with one little ingredient.

additional ingredient:
5 tbsp instant coffee granules

1. Follow the directions for the Vanilla Cake but in step #6, dissolve instant coffee granules into milk.

Chrysta's Favorite Frostings & Finishing Touches:
Cream Cheese Frosting, page 136
Chocolate Buttercream, page 127
Chocolate Covered Coffee Beans

Irish Cream Cake

On a trip to Dublin, I heard a rumor that 1/4 of Ireland's milk goes into the production of Irish Cream. I like to think of making this cake as my little way of supporting the Irish farmers.

1. Follow the directions for the Basic Vanilla Birthday Cake but in step #6 add the Irish Cream, along with the vanilla, to the milk.

additional ingredients:
1/2 C Irish Cream

Reduce milk to 3/4 cup.

Chrysta's Favorite Frostings & Finishing Touches:
Irish Cream Buttercream, page 128
Chocolate Buttercream, page 127

kiss my bundt

Miss Ellie's Eggnog Cake

My Aunt Eleanor, or Miss Ellie as we affectionately call her, is a feisty woman known to relish an occasional nip of brandy or rum. A few Christmases ago, she inspired me to create this eggnog cake. I call for rum in the recipe because it's commonly found in home liquor cabinets but you can also use brandy. But watch out, as little as one bite of this cake has been known to turn diners as feisty as Ellie!

additional ingredients:
1/8 tsp nutmeg
1/4 tsp cinnamon
3/4 C eggnog
2 tbsp rum or brandy
1/2 tsp rum extract, (optional)*

Reduce milk to 1/2 cup.

1. Follow the instructions for the Basic Vanilla Birthday Cake but add the cinnamon and nutmeg to the flour in step #2.

2. In step #6, combine the eggnog, rum and rum extract (optional) with 1/2 cup of milk.

   *The rum extract is optional but will add to the complexity of the cake's eggnog flavor.

Chrysta's Favorite Frostings & Finishing Touches:
Eggnog Buttercream, page 132

Coconut Cake

Some of my best childhood memories involve coconut cake. I still find it comforting to have a slice with a big glass of milk or cup of hot tea splashed with cream.

ingredients:

2 1/2 C flour

2 1/2 tsp baking powder

1/2 tsp salt

3/4 C unsalted butter

1 3/4 C sugar

3 eggs, room temperature

1 1/2 tsp vanilla

3/4 tsp coconut extract, (optional)*

3/4 C whole milk*

1/2 C coconut milk

1. Preheat oven to 350 degrees.

2. Sift flour and baking powder and salt together. Set aside.

3. Beat butter with an electric mixer until soft, about 2 minutes.

4. Slowly add the sugar. Mix for about 2 minutes.

5. Crack eggs into a separate bowl and add to batter one at a time. Then beat on medium speed for an additional 2 minutes.

6. Mix vanilla, coconut extract (optional) and the two milks together.

7. Beginning and ending with the flour, mix 1/3 of the flour into the wet mixture, then 1/2 of the milk, alternating until all ingredients are mixed.

8. 8. Transfer batter to cake pan(s) that have been coated with a baker's cooking spray that includes flour (or greased and floured), filling until cavity is about 3/4 full.

9. Bake cake(s) until an inserted toothpick or cake tester comes out clean—about 40 minutes for a big ol' bundt.

10. Invert cake(s) onto a cooling rack or serving plate. If cake resists, cool in the pan for 15 minutes before

*Coconut extract is optional but it will intensify the coconut flavor of the cake. For a more rich and exotic cake, you can omit the whole milk and use an additional 3/4 cup of coconut milk instead.

kiss my bundt

inverting. (If cake still resists, cool an additional 15 minutes in the pan.) Cool completely before frosting, at least 1 hour for a big ol' bundt.

Chrysta's Favorite Frostings & Finishing Touches:
Coconut Buttercream, page 129
Coconut Cream Cheese Frosting, page 136
White Chocolate Curls
Sweetened, Flake Coconut

Piña Colada Cake

To celebrate finishing graduate school, I took a trip to Mexico with my mom and some of our friends. On the trip, I learned that my mother loves Piña Coladas. To capture the memories of that wonderful trip, I created this cake. This one's for you, mom.

additional ingredients:
1/4 C rum

1 C canned crushed pineapple

Reduce the coconut extract (optional) to 1/2 tsp.*

Increase the whole milk to 1 cup.

Omit the coconut milk.

*Coconut extract is optional but it will intensify the tropical essence of the cake.

1. Follow the recipe for Coconut Cake, but in step #6, mix 1 cup of milk, 1/4 cup of rum, 1 1/2 tsp vanilla and 1/2 tsp coconut extract (optional).

2. Before step #8, put the crushed pineapple into a strainer and press out the liquid (too much liquid will make the batter runny and the cake will not bake properly). Once the liquid has been removed, fold pineapple into the batter.

Chrysta's Favorite Frostings & Finishing Touches:
Coconut Buttercream, page 129
Cream Cheese Frosting, page136
Coconut Cream Cheese Frosting, page 136
Piece of Fresh or Dried Pineapple

Banana Cake

I hate waste, which is one of the reasons I love this cake. Not only is it one of my bakery's best sellers but the recipe gives me something to do with overripe bananas. For a tropical banana flavor, top the cake with vanilla buttercream or cream cheese frosting. Or, try it with chocolate buttercream or glaze and it's like having a chocolate-covered banana.

1. Preheat oven to 350 degrees.

2. Sift flour and baking powder and salt together. Set aside.

3. Beat butter with an electric mixer until soft, about 2 minutes.

4. Slowly add the sugar. Mix for about 2 minutes.

5. Crack eggs into a separate bowl and add to batter one at a time. Then beat on medium speed for an additional 2 minutes.

6. Add vanilla and banana extract. (Yes, I know it smells like Banana Laffy Taffy. But you have to trust me. The extract amplifies the flavor of the real banana.)

ingredients:
2 1/2 C flour
2 1/2 tsp baking powder
1/2 tsp salt
3/4 C unsalted butter
1 3/4 C sugar
3 eggs, room temperature
1/2 tsp vanilla
1 tsp banana extract, (optional)*
1 1/4 C whole milk
1 banana, very ripe*

*If you don't dig the candy-like scent of banana extract, use two overripe bananas in the batter. The flavor will be less intense, more like banana bread.

kiss my bundt

7. Beginning and ending with the flour, mix 1/3 of the flour into the wet mixture, then 1/2 of the milk, alternating until all ingredients are mixed.

8. Take 1 whole banana and smash it into a small mixing bowl. When the consistency is fairly smooth and slightly liquid, fold into the vanilla batter.

9. Transfer batter to cake pan(s) that have been coated with a baker's cooking spray that includes flour (or greased and floured), filling until cavity is about 3/4 full.

10. Bake cake(s) until an inserted toothpick or cake tester comes out clean—about 40 minutes for a big ol' bundt.

11. Invert cake(s) onto a cooling rack or serving plate. If cake resists, cool in the pan for 15 minutes before inverting. (If cake still resists, cool an additional 15 minutes in the pan.) Cool completely before frosting, at least 1 hour for a big ol' bundt.

Chrysta's Favorite Frostings & Finishing Touches:
Vanilla Buttercream, page 127
Cream Cheese Frosting, page 136
Chocolate Buttercream, page 127
Chocolate Glaze, page 142
Dried Banana Chips

Blueberry Cake

Berries marry beautifully with the basic vanilla cake. You can try any berry you like but blueberry cake is a classic—especially around the Fourth of July. My head baker, Megan, and I once tried brightening the blueberry flavor with a tart twist of lime. To try this variation, add 2 tsp of lime zest to the batter and top with lime glaze.

1. Preheat oven to 350 degrees.

2. Sift flour and baking powder and salt together. Set aside.

3. Beat butter until soft, about 2 minutes.

4. Slowly add the sugar. Mix for about 2 minutes.

5. Crack eggs into a separate bowl and add to batter one at a time. Then beat on medium speed for an additional 2 minutes.

6. Add vanilla.

7. Beginning and ending with the flour, mix 1/3 of the flour into the wet mixture, then 1/2 of the milk, alternating until all ingredients are mixed.

8. Fold in cooled Blueberry Smash, mixing until entire batter turns purple.

9. Transfer batter to cake pan(s) that have been coated with a baker's cooking spray that includes flour (or greased and floured), filling until cavity is about 3/4 full.

10. Bake cake(s) until an inserted toothpick or cake tester comes out clean—about 40 minutes for a big ol' bundt.

ingredients:

2 1/2 C flour

2 1/2 tsp baking powder

1/2 tsp salt

3/4 C unsalted butter

1 3/4 C sugar

3 eggs, room temperature

1 1/2 tsp vanilla

1 1/4 C whole milk

1 batch Blueberry Smash, (recipe below)

kiss my bundt

11. Invert cake(s) onto a cooling rack or serving plate. If cake resists, cool in the pan for 15 minutes before inverting. (If cake still resists, cool an additional 15 minutes in the pan.) Cool completely before frosting, at least 1 hour for a big ol' bundt.

Chrysta's Favorite Frostings & Finishing Touches:
Vanilla Buttercream, page 127
Cream Cheese Frosting, page 136
Vanilla Glaze, page 139
Fresh Blueberries

Blueberry Smash

ingredients:
6 oz fresh blueberries*

2 tsp lemon juice

1/3 C granulated sugar

*In winter, you can use frozen blueberries. Replace 6 oz of fresh with 1 1/4 cup frozen blueberries. Thaw blueberries completely in a strainer so that excess water drains.

1. Take 6 oz (one small, standard container they sell at the markets) of blueberries. Cut the blueberries in half, then smash them with a fork or potato masher.

2. Add 2 tsp of lemon juice and the granulated sugar.

3. Bring to a boil, then drop to medium heat.

4. Cook until thickened, about 5-7 minutes on medium or medium-low heat.

5. Transfer to a small, heat-safe bowl and put in the fridge to cool (you cannot add hot smash to a batter).

Strawberry Cake

When I opened the bakery, this cake caused me some serious stress. I had it on the menu, but two weeks after we opened, I still couldn't get the recipe right. I wanted a cake with an intense strawberry flavor but fresh strawberries have a lot of water. I couldn't find a way of delivering strawberry flavor in a batter that wasn't too runny. The final recipe calls for cooking the berries to reduce the liquid and concentrate flavor. Strawberry gelatin enhances the cake's pink hue. Today, the recipe is one of the bakery's best sellers.

1. Preheat oven to 350 degrees.

2. Sift flour, baking powder, strawberry gelatin and salt together. Set aside.

3. Beat butter with an electric mixer at medium speed until creamy, about 2 minutes.

4. Slowly add the sugar. Beat on medium speed until the mixture is fluffy, about 2 minutes.

5. Crack eggs into a separate bowl and add to batter one at a time. Then beat on medium speed for an additional 2 minutes.

6. Fold in Strawberry Smash.

7. Add vanilla to the milk.

8. Beginning and ending with the flour, mix 1/3 of the flour into the wet mixture, then 1/2 of the milk, alternating until all ingredients are mixed.

ingredients:
2 1/2 C flour
2 1/2 tsp baking powder
3 tbsp strawberry gelatin
1/2 tsp salt
3/4 C unsalted butter
1 3/4 C sugar
3 eggs, room temperature
1 C Strawberry Smash, cool or at room temperature (see recipe page 40)
1 1/2 tsp vanilla
1 1/4 C whole milk

9. Transfer batter to cake pan(s) that have been coated with a baker's cooking spray that includes flour (or greased and floured), filling until cavity is about 3/4 full.

10. Bake cake(s) until an inserted toothpick or cake tester comes out clean—about 40 minutes for a big ol' bundt.

11. Invert cake(s) onto a cooling rack or serving plate. If cake resists, cool in the pan for 15 minutes before inverting. (If cake still resists, cool an additional 15 minutes in the pan.) Cool completely before frosting, at least 1 hour for a big ol' bundt.

Chrysta's Favorite Frostings & Finishing Touches:
Vanilla Buttercream, page 127
Cream Cheese Frosting, page 136
Straw-Raz Buttercream, page 134

Strawberry Smash

1. Toss the strawberries and the sugar together in a saucepan.

2. Add lemon juice and stir over medium-high heat.

3. Bring smash to a boil. Strawberries will begin to give off liquid as they cook. The mixture will begin to thicken as a result of the added sugar.

4. Once it reaches a boil, boil for 5 minutes, stirring occasionally.

5. Drop heat to medium-low and simmer mixture for about 25 minutes, stirring occasionally, as it thickens and reduces to desired smash consistence.

6. Transfer mixture to a heat-safe bowl and cool in the fridge. Cooled, the smash will have the consistency of strawberry jam or preserves. You must cool completely before using.

ingredients:
8 oz fresh strawberries, destemmed and sliced

1/2 C granulated white sugar

1/2 tsp lemon juice

Lemonade Picnic Cake

I grew up on lemonade, an absolute staple in Southern homes. There is nothing better for quenching thirst when the thermometer pushes 100. I created this cake to capture that refreshing quality in a dessert. And, as I did with lemonade when I grew bored of the basic recipe, I've played with berry-flavored variations of the cake, both of which are a hit in my house. (Only these days, I serve them with vodka-spiked lemonade.)

ingredients:

2 1/2 C flour

2 1/2 tsp baking powder

1/2 tsp salt

3/4 C unsalted butter

1 3/4 C sugar

3 eggs, room temperature

1/2 tsp vanilla

zest of 3 lemons

2 tsp lemon extract, (optional)*

1 1/4 C whole milk

* Lemon extract is optional, but it will intensify the lemon flavor of the cake.

1. Preheat oven to 350 degrees.

2. Sift flour and baking powder and salt together. Set aside.

3. Beat butter with an electric mixer until soft, about 2 minutes.

4. Slowly add the sugar. Beat on medium speed until the mixture is fluffy, about 2 minutes.

5. Crack eggs into a separate bowl and add to batter one at a time. Then beat on medium speed for an additional 2 minutes.

6. Add vanilla, zest and (optional) lemon extract.

7. Beginning and ending with the flour, mix 1/3 of the flour into the wet mixture, then 1/2 of the milk, alternating until all ingredients are mixed.

8. Transfer batter to cake pan(s) that have been coated with a baker's cooking spray that includes flour (or greased and floured), filling until cavity is about 3/4 full.

9. Bake cake(s) until an inserted toothpick or cake tester comes out clean—about 40 minutes for a big ol' bundt.

10. Invert cake(s) onto a cooling rack or serving plate. If cake resists, cool in the pan for 15 minutes before inverting. (If cake still resists, cool an additional 15 minutes in the pan.) Cool completely before frosting, at least 1 hour for a big ol' bundt.

Chrysta's Favorite Frostings & Finishing Touches:
Lemon Buttercream, page 130
Citrus Buttercream, page 131
Lemon Gummy Fruit Slices

Strawberry Lemonade Picnic Cake

1. Add 2 tbsp strawberry-flavored gelatin to the dry ingredients in step #2.

2. In step #6, add strawberry smash to the vanilla, zest, lemon extract (optional) and cup of milk.

additional ingredients:

2 tbsp strawberry-flavored gelatin

3 tbsp Strawberry Smash, page 40

Reduce milk to 1 cup.

Chrysta's Favorite Frostings & Finishing Touches:
Plain
Lemon Buttercream, page 130
Lemon Glaze, page 140

Raspberry Lemonade Picnic Cake

additional ingredients:
1 tbsp raspberry-flavored gelatin

3 tbsp raspberry purée, (see recipe below)

Reduce milk to 1 cup.

1. Add 1 tbsp raspberry-flavored gelatin to the dry ingredients in step #2.

2. In step #6, add raspberry puree to the vanilla, zest, lemon extract (optional) to 1 cup of milk.

Chrysta's Favorite Frostings & Finishing Touches:
Plain
Lemon Buttercream, page130
Lemon Glaze, page 140

Raspberry Purée

ingredients:
1/2 pt raspberries

2 tsp lemon juice

1/3 C sugar

1. In a small saucepan, mash the raspberries. Add lemon juice and sugar. Stir to incorporate.

2. Bring to a boil. This helps release the raspberry juice.

3. One the mixture reaches a boil, remove from heat and transfer to a blender or food processor. Puree until smooth.

4. Pour the puree through a sieve/strainer so the raspberry sauce comes through and the seeds are left behind.

Use leftover raspberry puree as the foundation for a raspberry-flavored lemonade or cocktail. Or transfer to a ketchup bottle and use as a sauce for decorating dessert plates.

Lime Basil Cake

One day I decided to take my Southern recipe and mixed it up South Asian-style. It took me a few tries to realize the trick to using savory herbs in a cake but I'll share it with you for no extra charge: To fully integrate the flavors, it is important to finely mince the basil and let it steep in the milk so that the basil release its oil. If you fail to follow this step, you'll wind up with a cake that tastes too heavily of the herb.

ingredients:

1/3 C packed basil leaves, (sans stems)

1 1/4 C whole milk

2 1/2 C flour

2 1/2 tsp baking powder

1/2 tsp salt

3/4 C unsalted butter

1 3/4 C sugar

3 eggs, room temperature

1/2 tsp vanilla

1 tbsp lime juice

1 tsp lime oil, (or zest of 4 limes if you don't have lime oil)

1. Stack basil leaves on top of one another and finely slice with a very sharp knife. Then finely mince, making clean cuts so as not to bruise the basil too much. Add basil to the milk. Set aside for 10 minutes. (It is VERY important to do this step first, so that the basil oil has time to mix with the milk.)

2. Preheat oven to 350 degrees.

3. Sift flour and baking powder and salt together. Set aside.

4. Beat butter with an electric mixer until soft, about 2 minutes.

5. Slowly add the sugar. Mix for about 2 minutes.

6. After you've cracked eggs into a separate bowl to ensure no shells, add to mixer one at a time. Then beat for an additional 2 minutes.

7. Add vanilla, lime juice and lime oil (or the zest of four limes).

8. Beginning and ending with the flour, mix 1/3 of the

flour into the wet mixture, then 1/2 of the milk, alternating until all ingredients are mixed.

9. Transfer batter to cake pan(s) that have been coated with a baker's cooking spray that includes flour (or greased and floured), filling until cavity is about 3/4 full.

10. Bake cake(s) until an inserted toothpick or cake tester comes out clean—about 40 minutes for a big ol' bundt.

11. Invert cake(s) onto a cooling rack or serving plate. If cake resists, cool in the pan for 15 minutes before inverting. (If cake still resists, cool an additional 15 minutes in the pan.) Cool completely before frosting, at least 1 hour for a big ol' bundt.

Chrysta's Favorite Frostings & Finishing Touches:
Plain
Vanilla Buttercream, page 127
Lime Glaze, page 140

Lemon Basil Cake

additional ingredients:
zest of 1 lemon

I tbsp lemon juice

1 tsp lemon extract* (optional)
Omit lime juice and lime oil or zest.

*The natural extract is optional but will intensify the lemon flavor of the cake.

1. Follow method for lime basil, adding the lemon zest, lemon juice and lemon extract instead of the lime in step #7.

Chrysta's Favorite Frostings & Finishing Touches:
Plain
Vanilla Buttercream, page127
Lemon Glaze, page 140

Citrilicious Cake

I've lived in Florida and I've lived in California. I have had more than my share of experience with lemons, oranges and limes. I've grown to absolutely love the bright and tart notes citrus fruits bring to my batters. This cake utilizes all of the "big three" to pack the biggest, tangiest punch of all my citrus-inspired cakes. It's citrus. It's delicious. It's Citrilicious!

1. Preheat oven to 350 degrees.

2. Sift flour and baking powder and salt together. Set aside.

3. Beat butter until soft, about 2 minutes.

4. Slowly add the sugar. Mix for about 2 minutes.

5. Crack eggs into a separate bowl and add to batter one at a time. Then beat on medium speed for an additional 2 minutes.

6. Add zests and extracts.

7. Beginning and ending with the flour, mix 1/3 of the flour into the wet mixture, then 1/2 of the milk, alternating until all ingredients are mixed.

8. Transfer batter to cake pan(s) that have been coated with a baker's cooking spray that includes flour (or greased and floured), filling until cavity is about 3/4 full.

9. Bake cake(s) until an inserted toothpick or cake tester comes out clean—about 40 minutes for a big ol' bundt.

ingredients:

2 1/2 C flour

2 1/2 tsp baking powder

1/2 tsp salt

3/4 C unsalted butter

3/4 C sugar

3 eggs, room temperature

zest of 2 medium oranges

zest of 1 medium lemon

zest of 1 1/2 limes

1 tsp pure orange extract, (optional)*

1/2 tsp pure lemon extract, (optional)*

1 1/4 C whole milk

* The natural extracts are optional but will intensify the citrus flavors of the cake.

10. Invert cake(s) onto a cooling rack or serving plate. If cake resists, cool in the pan for 15 minutes before inverting. (If cake still resists, cool an additional 15 minutes in the pan.) Cool completely before frosting, at least 1 hour for a big ol' bundt.

Chrysta's Favorite Frostings & Finishing Touches:
Vanilla Buttercream, page 127
Lemon Buttercream, page 130
Orange Buttercream, page 130
Citrus Buttercream, page 131
Lemon Glaze, page 140
Lime Glaze, page 140
Citrus Gummy Fruit Slices

Margarita Cake

Some of the cakes I bake come from family tradition; others have a great story behind their evolution. This one's a little simpler. I love the south-of-the-border flavors in a Margarita. So I invented a cake to capture its essence. (Besides, what else is a cake baker going to serve for Cinco de Mayo?)

1. Preheat oven to 350 degrees.
2. Sift flour and baking powder and salt together. Set aside.
3. Beat butter with an electric mixer at medium speed until soft, about 2 minutes.

ingredients:

- 2 1/2 C flour
- 2 1/2 tsp baking powder
- 1/2 tsp salt
- 3/4 C unsalted butter
- 1 3/4 C sugar
- 3 eggs, room temperature
- 3/4 C whole milk
- 1/2 tsp vanilla
- 1 tsp orange zest, about the zest of 1/2 small orange
- zest of 1 medium lime
- 1/3 C liquid Margarita mix
- 1/4 C tequila, (optional)*

*You can make this cake without the alcohol, but tequila will give you the most authentic flavor.

4. Slowly add the sugar. Beat on medium speed until the mixture is fluffy, about 2 minutes.

5. Crack eggs into a separate bowl and add to batter one at a time. Then beat on medium speed for an additional two minutes.

6. Mix milk, vanilla, orange zest, lime zest, Margarita mix and tequila together. (Note: mixture will begin to curdle. Don't worry, this is normal).

7. Beginning and ending with the flour, mix 1/3 of the flour into the wet mixture, then 1/2 of the milk mixture, alternating until all ingredients are mixed.

8. Transfer batter to cake pan(s) that have been coated with a baker's cooking spray that includes flour (or greased and floured), filling until cavity is about 3/4 full.

9. Bake cake(s) until an inserted toothpick or cake tester comes out clean—about 40 minutes for a big ol' bundt.

10. Invert cake(s) onto a cooling rack or serving plate. If cake resists, cool in the pan for 15 minutes before inverting. (If cake still resists, cool an additional 15 minutes in the pan.) Cool completely before frosting, at least 1 hour for a big ol' bundt.

Chrysta's Favorite Frostings & Finishing Touches:

Margarita Buttercream, page 131
Lime Gummy Fruit Slices

Fresh Ginger Cake

In the world of cake, ginger is most often used in combination with molasses and spice to make gingerbread. This ginger cake explores fresh-grated ginger's lighter side in a delicate, butter-based cake. The trick is to let the ginger infuse the milk with its faintly spicy flavor and then blend it into the cake for a subtly exotic taste.

To Prepare Ginger

Peel the paper, brown skin from the ginger. Grate the exposed root by hand to obtain 1 tbsp fresh ginger. (You can wrap any leftover root in parchment paper and then a plastic sandwich bag to preserve.)

1. Preheat oven to 350 degrees.

2. Add grated ginger and vanilla to milk. Set aside.

3. Sift flour, baking powder and salt together. Set aside.

4. Beat butter with an electric mixer at medium speed until creamy, about 2 minutes.

5. Slowly add the sugar. Beat on medium speed until the mixture is fluffy, about 2 minutes.

6. Crack eggs into a separate bowl and add to batter one at a time. Then beat on medium speed for an additional two minutes.

7. Beginning and ending with the flour, mix 1/3 of the flour into the wet mixture at a low speed, then 1/2 of the milk, alternating until all ingredients are mixed.

ingredients:
1 tbsp of freshly-grated ginger, approx a 2" - 3" section of fresh ginger root
1 1/2 tsp vanilla
1 1/4 C whole milk
2 1/2 C flour
2 1/2 tsp baking powder
1/2 tsp salt
3/4 C unsalted butter
1 3/4 C sugar
3 eggs, room temperature

kiss my bundt

8. Transfer batter to cake pan(s) that have been coated with a baker's cooking spray that includes flour (or greased and floured), filling until cavity is about 3/4 full.

9. Bake cake(s) until an inserted toothpick or cake tester comes out clean—about 40 minutes for a big ol' bundt.

10. Invert cake(s) onto a cooling rack or serving plate. If cake resists, cool in the pan for 15 minutes before inverting. (If cake still resists, cool an additional 15 minutes in the pan.) Cool completely before frosting, at least 1 hour for a big ol' bundt.

Chrysta's Favorite Frostings & Finishing Touches:
Vanilla Buttercream, page 127
Candied Ginger

Lemon Ginger Cake

additional ingredients:
2 tsp lemon zest

1. Follow the recipe for Ginger Cake, adding 2 tsp of freshly grated lemon zest to the recipe in step #2.

Chrysta's Favorite Frostings & Finishing Touches:
Plain
Vanilla Buttercream, page 127
Lemon Buttercream, page 130

Strawberry Ginger Cake

1. Follow the recipe for Ginger Cake but in step #2, add 1/3 cup Strawberry Smash with the grated ginger and vanilla to 1 cup whole milk.

additional ingredient:
1/3 C Strawberry Smash

Reduce milk to 1 cup.

Chrysta's Favorite Frostings & Finishing Touches:
Plain
Vanilla Buttercream, page 127

Almond Cake

I love almond (the nut, the flavoring *and* the cake). The simple addition of ground almonds and extract take the cake recipe from vanilla to *va va voom*. I like the cake plain, but with cream cheese frosting, it becomes my partner of choice to a mug of hot chocolate.

1. Take the 2/3 cup almonds and grind them in a food processor with about 2 tbsp of white granulated sugar. (Or use 1/2 cup pre-packaged almond meal and combine with sugar).
2. Preheat oven to 350 degrees.
3. Sift flour and baking powder and salt together. Stir in the 1/2 cup of ground almonds. Set aside.
4. With an electric mixer, cream butter for 2 minutes.
5. Slowly add the 1 3/4 cups of sugar. Mix for an additional 2 minutes.

ingredients:
2/3 C almonds or 1/2 C almond meal
1 3/4 C plus 2 tbsp sugar
2 C flour
2 1/2 tsp baking powder
1/2 tsp salt
3/4 C unsalted butter
3 eggs, room temperature
1/2 tsp vanilla extract
1/2 tsp almond extract
1 1/4 C whole milk

kiss my bundt

6. Crack eggs into a separate bowl and add to batter one at a time. Then beat on medium speed for an additional 2 minutes.

7. Add vanilla and almond extracts to the milk.

8. Beginning and ending with the flour, mix 1/3 of the flour into the wet mixture, then 1/2 of the milk, alternating until all ingredients are mixed.

9. Transfer batter to cake pan(s) that have been coated with a baker's cooking spray that includes flour (or greased and floured), filling until cavity is about 3/4 full.

10. Bake cake(s) until an inserted toothpick or cake tester comes out clean—about 40 minutes for a big ol' bundt.

11. Invert cake(s) onto a cooling rack or serving plate. If cake resists, cool in the pan for 15 minutes before inverting. (If cake still resists, cool an additional 15 minutes in the pan.) Cool completely before frosting, at least 1 hour for a big ol' bundt.

Chrysta's Favorite Frostings & Finishing Touches:
Plain
Vanilla Buttercream, page 127
Cream Cheese Frosting, page 136
Vanilla Glaze, page 139
Almond Glaze, page 140

Aphrodisiac Cherry Vanilla Almond Cake

Ground almonds, fresh cherries and vanilla marry in an aphrodisiac *ménage á trois*. At the bakery, this cake debuted on Valentine's Day 2009 to raves.

1. Preheat oven to 350 degrees.

2. Sift flour, baking powder and salt together. Set aside.

3. Beat butter until soft, about 2 minutes.

4. Slowly add the sugar. Beat on medium speed until the mixture is fluffy, about 2 minutes.

5. Crack eggs into a separate bowl and add to batter one at a time. Then beat on medium speed for an additional 2 minutes.

6. Add vanilla and almond extract.

7. Beginning and ending with the flour, mix 1/3 of the flour into the wet mixture, then 1/2 of the milk, alternating until all ingredients are mixed.

8. Toss cherries with the ground almonds then fold cherry mixture into the batter, being careful to fully incorporate the cherry juice.

9. Transfer batter to cake pan(s) that have been coated with a baker's cooking spray that includes flour (or greased and floured), filling until cavity is about 3/4 full.

10. Bake cake(s) until an inserted toothpick or cake tester comes out clean—about 40 minutes for a big ol' bundt.

ingredients:
2 1/2 C flour
2 1/2 tsp baking powder
1/2 tsp salt
3/4 C unsalted butter
1 3/4 C sugar
3 eggs, room temperature
1/2 tsp vanilla extract
1/2 tsp almond extract
1 1/4 C whole milk
1 C fresh, black cherries, pitted and coarsely-chopped
3 tbsp ground almonds or almond meal

11. Invert cake(s) onto a cooling rack or serving plate. If cake resists, cool in the pan for 15 minutes before inverting. (If cake still resists, cool an additional 15 minutes in the pan.) Cool completely before frosting, at least 1 hour for a big ol' bundt.

Chrysta's Favorite Frostings & Finishing Touches:
Plain
Vanilla Buttercream, page 127
Vanilla Glaze, page 139
Almond Glaze, page 140

Pistachio Cream Cake

When I quit my job and made the leap to bakery owner, my friend Michelle had her mom Linda bring a farewell bundt to my office. It was a bundt layer cake—which I had never experienced before—a stack of cake and pistachio cream. A year later, I found myself craving the cake so intensely that I decided to reverse engineer the cake from memory – and the remake was as good as the original. But it does require one special trick that took me a couple of tries to master. To cut layers into your bundt, put down the knife and try using unflavored dental floss. Tie the floss around the cake as if you were tying a bow and gently pull it through. This method cuts layers cleanly and easily. Top with a dusting of powdered sugar and you'll have one of the prettiest cakes in the book.

1. Preheat oven to 350 degrees.

2. Sift flour, baking powder and salt together. Stir in pistachio pudding and set aside.

3. Using an electric mixer, beat butter until soft, about 2 minutes.

4. Slowly add the sugar. Beat on medium speed until the mixture is fluffy, about 2 minutes.

5. Crack the eggs into a separate bowl.

6. After you've cracked eggs into a separate bowl to ensure no shells, add to mixer one at a time. Then beat for an additional 2 minutes.

7. Add vanilla.

8. Beginning and ending with the flour, mix 1/3 of the flour into the wet mixture, then 1/2 of the milk, alternating until all ingredients are mixed.

9. Transfer batter to cake pan(s) that have been coated with a baker's cooking spray that includes flour (or greased and floured), filling until cavity is about 3/4 full.

10. Bake cake(s) until an inserted toothpick or cake tester comes out clean—about 40 minutes for a big ol' bundt.

11. Invert cake(s) onto a cooling rack or serving plate. If cake resists, cool in the pan for 15 minutes before inverting. (If cake still resists, cool an additional 15 minutes in the pan.) Cool completely before frosting, at least 1 hour for a big ol' bundt.

This cake is great plain but is perfect frosted with layers of Pistachio Cream (next page).

ingredients:

2 1/2 C flour

2 1/2 tsp baking powder

1/2 tsp salt

2 boxes (3.4 or 3.5 oz) instant pistachio pudding mix

3/4 C unsalted butter

1 3/4 C sugar

3 eggs, room temperature

1 1/2 tsp vanilla

1 1/4 C whole milk

kiss my bundt

Pistachio Cream

ingredients:

2 boxes (3.4 or 3.5 ounce) instant pistachio pudding

2 C whipped cream, (see page 144 for instructions on whipping cream)

Gently fold pistachio pudding into whipped cream, mixing until completely incorporated.

Frosting the Pistachio Cake with Pistachio Cream

1. When cakes have cooled completely, slice into layers. Cut mini bundt and baby bundt cakes in half and cut the big ol' bundt into 3 layers. (See a tip below for cutting layers.)*

2. Set layers aside.

3. You can spread as much pistachio cream as you'd like on each layer, however, I recommend about 2-3 tbsp for a mini bundt and about 4-6 tbsp for a baby bundt. And, I like about 3/4 cup of cream on each big ol' bundt layer.

Tip for cutting the big ol' bundt into layers:

First, stick a toothpick horizontally into the side of the cake approximately 1/3 from the top of the cake. Then stick a toothpick approximately 1/3 from the bottom of the cake. These are your markers for cutting the layers. If you want more layers, mark them with evenly-spaced toothpicks. Then take a 20-inch piece of unflavored, wax-free dental floss. Wrap the floss around the cake just above your toothpick marker. Then cross the floss as if you were tying a bow. Keep pulling the floss until the floss has cut the entire first layer. Repeat until all your layers have been cut.

Champagne Celebration Cake

Ok, I would *never* say a cake is better than a bottle of Champagne. But if you want to find a dessert worthy of your best bottle of bubbly...here it is. It's not bragging, really, I just sincerely believe this is a perfect cake for any celebration, especially served alongside a crisp, chilled sparkling wine. When I bake it for a party, I like to make a little extra just for me. My "day after" cake, I like this cake almost better the second day.

1. Preheat oven to 350 degrees.

2. Sift flour and baking powder and salt together. Set aside.

3. Beat butter until soft, about 2 minutes.

4. Slowly add the sugar. Mix for about 2 minutes.

5. Crack eggs into a separate bowl and add to batter one at a time. Then beat on medium speed for an additional 2 minutes.

6. Combine vanilla, Champagne, and milk. The milk will start to curdle. Don't worry, this is normal. The acidity of the Champagne and the carbonation are reacting with the dairy.

7. Beginning and ending with the flour, mix 1/3 of the flour into the wet mixture, then 1/2 of the milk, alternating until all ingredients are mixed.

8. Fold 5 tbsp Champagne Syrup into the batter.

ingredients:

2 1/2 C flour

2 1/2 tsp baking powder

1/2 tsp salt

3/4 C unsalted butter

1 3/4 C sugar

3 eggs, room temperature

1 1/2 tsp vanilla

1/2 C Champagne or sparkling wine

3/4 C whole milk

5 tbsp Champagne Syrup, (see recipe below)

9. Transfer batter to cake pan(s) that have been coated with a baker's cooking spray that includes flour (or greased and floured), filling until cavity is about 3/4 full.

10. Bake cake(s) until an inserted toothpick or cake tester comes out clean—about 40 minutes for a big ol' bundt.

11. Invert cake(s) onto a cooling rack or serving plate. If cake resists, cool in the pan for 15 minutes before inverting. (If cake still resists, cool an additional 15 minutes in the pan.) Cool completely before frosting, at least 1 hour for a big ol' bundt.

Chrysta's Favorite Frostings & Finishing Touches:
Champagne Buttercream, page 132

Champagne Syrup

ingredients:
1/2 C Champagne or sparkling wine

1/2 C granulated sugar

1. In a small saucepan, bring Champagne and sugar to a boil.

2. Once the sugar dissolves and the mixture is clear, boil 1 additional minute.

3. Reduce heat and simmer for 2 minutes.

4. Transfer to a heat-safe bowl and place in the refrigerator to cool. You have to cool the syrup before adding it to the batter or frosting.

Riesling, Apricot and Honey Aphrodisiac Cake

Combining Riesling wine with fresh apricots and a kiss of honey, this cake evokes Old World romanticism. Its flavors are buttery and complex but subtle, the perfect sort of sweet to serve to someone sweet. *(It works particularly well as a morning after cake, if you know what I mean.)*

For the apricots:

1. Take the apricots and soak overnight in Riesling. Use just enough wine to cover the apricots, about 1 cup.

2. After soaking (at least 6 hours), drain apricots and purée using a blender or food processor. This should produce 1/2 c puree, depending on the size of your apricots but measure to double check.

3. Reserve 1/4 cup of the soaking wine for the cake batter.

For the cake:

1. Preheat oven to 350 degrees.

2. Sift flour and baking powder and salt together. Set aside.

3. Beat butter with an electric mixer at medium speed until creamy, about 2 minutes.

4. Slowly add the sugar. Beat on medium speed until the mixture is fluffy, about 2 minutes.

5. Add 1/2 cup of apricot puree to the sugar and butter mixture. Then, add the honey.

ingredients:
4 oz fresh apricots
1 C semi-sweet Riesling wine, (used to soak apricots)
2 1/2 C flour
2 1/2 tsp baking powder
1/2 tsp salt
3/4 C unsalted butter
1 3/4 C sugar
1/3 C honey
3 eggs, room temperature
1/2 tsp vanilla
1 C milk
1/4 C apricot soaking wine

6. Crack eggs into a separate bowl and add to batter one at a time. Then beat on medium speed for an additional 2 minutes.

7. Add vanilla extract and apricot soaking wine to the milk.

8. Beginning and ending with the flour, mix 1/3 of the flour into the wet mixture, then 1/2 of the milk, alternating until all ingredients are mixed.

9. Transfer batter to cake pan(s) that have been coated with a baker's cooking spray that includes flour (or greased and floured), filling until cavity is about 3/4 full.

10. Bake cake(s) until an inserted toothpick or cake tester comes out clean—about 40 minutes for a big ol' bundt.

11. Invert cake(s) onto a cooling rack or serving plate. If cake resists, cool in the pan for 15 minutes before inverting. (If cake still resists, cool an additional 15 minutes in the pan.) Cool completely before frosting, at least 1 hour for a big ol' bundt.

Chrysta's Favorite Frostings & Finishing Touches:
Plain
Vanilla Buttercream, page 127
Cream Cheese Frosting, page 136
Vanilla Glaze, page 139

Pineapple Upside Down Cake

When I added traditional Pineapple Upside Down to the bakery's menu, our customers went berserk. Patrons would share their stories about the first time they had this cake or how, when they were young, this was the cake their mother would bake for them. Although at Kiss My Bundt I don't dare veer from the traditional ingredients, for this book I've updated the flavor slightly, swapping out the maraschinos for richly flavored-dark cherries.

1. Preheat oven to 350 degrees.

2. Sift flour and baking powder and salt together. Set aside.

3. Beat butter with an electric mixer at medium speed until creamy, about 2 minutes.

4. Slowly add the sugar. Beat on medium speed until the mixture is fluffy, about 2 minutes.

5. Crack eggs into a separate bowl and add to batter one at a time. Then beat on medium speed for an additional 2 minutes.

6. Add vanilla to milk.

7. Beginning and ending with the flour, mix 1/3 of the flour into the wet mixture, then 1/2 of the milk, alternating until all ingredients are mixed.

8. Coat pan(s) with a baker's cooking spray that includes flour (or grease and flour).

ingredients:
2 1/2 C flour

2 1/2 tsp baking powder

1/2 tsp salt

3/4 C unsalted butter

1 3/4 C sugar

3 eggs, room temperature

1 1/2 tsp vanilla

1 1/4 C whole milk

1 can pineapple rings, drained

5 frozen or canned dark cherries, pitted and halved

for the caramel:
3/4 C butter

1 tbsp corn syrup

1 C brown sugar, packed

9. Line the bottom of the pan with pineapple rings (6-12 rings for a big 'ol bundt depending on your bundt pan's shape). For cupcake-sized bundts, chop pineapple and put a cherry slice in the bottom of each cup topped with 2 tsp of the pineapple.

10. Put a half cherry in the center of each pineapple ring.

11. Make the caramel by combining the butter, corn syrup and brown sugar in a saucepan over medium heat, stirring until mixture is smooth.

12. Pour the warm caramel over the pineapple and cherries at the bottom of the pan. For cupcake-sized bundts, use 1 tbsp and 2 tsp of caramel per cake. (Use care in handling caramel, it will burn).

13. Transfer batter to cake pan(s), filling until cavity is about 3/4 full.

14. Bake cake(s) until an inserted toothpick or cake tester comes out clean—about 40 minutes for a big ol' bundt.

15. Invert cake(s) onto a cooling rack or serving plate. If cake resists, cool in the pan for 15 minutes before inverting. (If cake still resists, cool an additional 15 minutes in the pan.) Cool completely before frosting, at least 1 hour for a big ol' bundt.

*The caramel may bubble out of the cake pan. For easy cleanup, line the oven rack with a sheet of aluminum foil.

• 3 •
Pound Bundts

Pound cakes should be made in a bundt pan. (Ok, it isn't a rule, per se, but it's my belief and I'm sticking to it!)

Pound cakes are the dense, buttery cakes prevalent in the Southern U.S. The cake was dubbed "pound" because, originally, the cakes were made from a pound of flour, a pound of sugar, a pound of butter and a pound of eggs. Today, pound cakes often stray from these proportions (after all, that's *a lot* of batter). However, if the recipe doesn't produce that dense, buttery texture, it's not a pound.

A child of the South, I remember pound cakes at nearly every family event. After a heavy meal, a pound cake for dessert offered an end-of-meal sweet without overwhelming layers of fudge or frosting. In fact, that's one of pound cakes' finest features. They are incredibly satisfying "as is"—perfect served plain and unadorned. Southerners, myself included, never frost a pound cake with a cream cheese or buttercream frosting. Instead, we serve pounds plain, finished with a light glaze or topped with a dollop of whipped cream, and maybe a side of fresh berries.

Note: The pound cake recipes in this chapter are intended only for a 10-12 cup, (big ol' bundt) pan. Made in individual pans, the cakes just don't create that wonderful pound cake density and texture.

Pure Joy Pound Cake
For big ol' bundt pan only

My Aunt Dia sparked my passion for baking when I was just a youngster. But around the age of eight, I discovered that this woman with whom I had spent hours bonding over batter wasn't a "Dia" at all. Her real name was Joy. (Dia wasn't any part of her legal name but for some reason, that's what we called her.) I named this classic pound cake after Joy, aka Aunt Dia. I like to serve the way she would, with a dusting of powdered sugar and a side of whipped cream and fresh berries. Try it with a glass of sparkling wine and you too will be filled with pure joy.

1. Preheat oven to 350 degrees.

2. Beat butter with an electric mixer on a medium-slow speed while slowly adding sugar. Continue until mixture is fluffy, about 3 minutes.

3. Crack eggs into a separate bowl and add to batter one at a time. Then beat on medium speed for an additional 2 minutes.

4. In another bowl, sift together flour, baking powder, and salt. Set aside.

5. Add the vanilla extract to the milk.

6. Turn the mixer speed to low. Beginning and ending with the flour, add 1/3 of the flour to the mixing bowl, then 1/2 of the milk mixture, alternating until all ingredients are mixed.

7. Pour batter into a big ol' bundt pan that has been coated with a baker's cooking spray that includes flour (or greased and floured).

8. Bake until just done, about 55 minutes or until inserted cake tester or skewer comes out clean—check cake often to be sure not to overbake.

9. Invert cake onto a cooling rack or serving plate. If cake resists, cool in the pan for 15 minutes before inverting. (If cake still resists, cool an additional 15 minutes in the pan.) Cool completely before glazing, at least 1 hour.

ingredients:

1 1/2 C unsalted butter

3 C sugar

5 eggs, room temperature

3 C flour

1 1/2 tsp baking powder

1/4 tsp salt

2 C whole milk

1 tsp vanilla

Chrysta's Recommended Finishing Touches:
Dusting of Powdered Sugar
Fresh Berries and Whipped Cream, page 144
Vanilla Glaze, page 139

Bourbon Pound Cake
For big ol' bundt pan only

Bourbon is the drink of choice for one of my best friends, so I've gotten to know the drink through his guidance. I was a little nervous the first time I made this cake for him but he loved it. And it remains one of his favorites. The cake has bourbon in the batter and is finished with bourbon glaze for an extra layer of whiskey flavor. To downplay the bourbon in the cake, omit the bourbon glaze and enjoy it plain. Or if you're ready to feel some heat, pair the glazed pound cake with bourbon on the rocks.

1. Preheat oven to 350 degrees.

2. Beat butter with an electric mixer on a medium-slow speed while slowly adding sugar. Continue until mixture is fluffy, about 3 minutes.

3. Crack eggs into a separate bowl and add to batter one at a time. Then beat on medium speed for an additional 2 minutes.

4. In another bowl, sift together flour, baking powder and salt. Set aside.

5. Add bourbon and vanilla to the milk.

6. Turn the mixer speed to low. Beginning and ending with the flour, add 1/3 of the flour to the mixing bowl, then 1/2 of the milk mixture, alternating until all ingredients are mixed.

7. Pour batter into a big ol' bundt pan that has been coated with a baker's cooking spray that includes flour (or greased and floured).

8. Bake until just done, about 55 minutes or until inserted cake tester or skewer comes out clean—check cake often to be sure not to overbake.

9. Invert cake onto a cooling rack or serving plate. If cake resists, cool in the pan for 15 minutes before inverting. (If cake still resists, cool an additional 15 minutes in the pan.) Cool completely before glazing, at least 1 hour.

ingredients:

1 1/2 C unsalted butter
3 C sugar
5 eggs, room temperature
3 C flour
1 1/2 tsp baking powder
1/4 tsp salt
1/4 C bourbon
1/2 tsp vanilla
1 3/4 C whole milk

Chrysta's Recommended Finishing Touches:
Plain
Bourbon Glaze, page 141

Rum Pound Cake
For big ol' bundt pan only

Caribbean rum is a popular ingredient in cooking where I grew up in Florida. I like baking with dark rum because I find its flavor subtler than that of the other alcohols I use in baking (like whiskey). And there's something innate to rum that works perfectly with sweet, butter and/or cream flavors. Try pairing this cake with a steaming cup of Jamaican Blue Mountain java. Or, for celebrations, there is nothing more appropriate to dress up rum cake than a round of pina coladas.

additional ingredient:
1/4 C dark rum

Omit the bourbon.

1. Follow the recipe for the Bourbon Pound Cake, except, in step #5, substitute 1/4 cup of the rum for the bourbon.

Chrysta's Recommended Finishing Touches:
Plain
Rum Glaze, page 141

Sour Cream Pound Cake
For big ol' bundt pan only

Butter and sour cream can make almost anything better. Ask a potato. The sour cream in this cake gives it a slight tang and creaminess that sets it apart from a plain pound cake. I love to serve it with whipped cream and berries, almost like a strawberry shortcake.

1. Preheat oven to 350 degrees.

2. Beat butter with an electric mixer on a medium-slow speed while slowly adding sugar. Continue until mixture is fluffy, about 3 minutes.

3. Crack eggs into a separate bowl and add to batter one at a time. Then beat on medium speed for an additional 2 minutes.

4. In another bowl, sift together flour, baking soda and salt. Set aside.

5. Add vanilla to sour cream.

6. Turn the mixer speed to low. Beginning and ending with the flour, add 1/3 of the flour to the mixing bowl, then 1/2 of the sour cream mixture, alternating until all ingredients are mixed.

7. Pour batter into a big ol' bundt pan that has been coated with a baker's cooking spray that includes flour (or greased and floured).

ingredients:

1 1/4 C unsalted butter

3 C sugar

6 eggs, room temperature

3 C flour

1/2 tsp baking soda

1/2 tsp salt

1 tsp vanilla

1 1/4 C sour cream

kiss my bundt

8. Bake until just done, about 55 minutes or until inserted cake tester or skewer comes out clean—check cake often to be sure not to overbake.

9. Invert cake onto a cooling rack or serving plate. If cake resists, cool in the pan for 15 minutes before inverting. (If cake still resists, cool an additional 15 minutes in the pan.)

Chrysta's Recommended Finishing Touches:
Plain
Sliced with Fresh Berries and a Dollop of Whipped Cream, page 144

Lemon Pound Cake
For big ol' bundt pan only

I think the lemon just might be a perfect food. Its flavors offer both intense sour and sweetness, one of my favorite combinations. Lemon pound cake on its own plays up the sweet side of the citrus but drizzled with the lemon glaze, the cake offers that taste bud-teasing interplay I crave.

1. Preheat oven to 350 degrees.

2. Beat butter with an electric mixer on a medium-slow speed while slowly adding sugar. Continue until mixture is fluffy, about 3 minutes.

3. Crack eggs into a separate bowl and add to batter one at a time. Then beat on medium speed for an additional 2 minutes.

4. In another bowl, sift together flour, baking soda and salt. Set aside.

5. Mix together lemon juice, lemon zest, vanilla, sour cream and milk.

6. Turn the mixer speed to low. Beginning and ending with the flour, add 1/3 of the flour into the mixing bowl, then 1/2 of the sour cream mixture, alternating until all ingredients are mixed.

7. Pour batter into a big ol' bundt pan that has been greased and floured.

8. Bake until just done, about 55 minutes or until inserted cake tester or skewer comes out clean—check cake often to be sure not to overbake.

9. Invert cake onto a cooling rack or serving plate. If cake resists, cool in the pan for 15 minutes before inverting. (If cake still resists, cool an additional 15 minutes in the pan.) Cool completely before glazing, at least 1 hour.

ingredients:

1 1/4 C unsalted butter

3 C sugar

6 eggs, room temperature

3 C flour

1/2 tsp baking soda

1/2 tsp salt

1/4 C fresh lemon juice

5 tbsp grated lemon zest (about the zest of 4-5 average lemons)

1/4 tsp vanilla extract

1/2 C sour cream

1/4 C whole milk

Chrysta's Recommended Finishing Touches:
Plain
Lemon Glaze, page 140

Orange Dream Pound Cake
For big ol' bundt pan only

additional ingredients:

5 tbsp orange zest (about the zest of 3-4 average oranges)

1/4 C fresh squeezed orange juice

Omit the lemon juice and zest.

A few years ago, my friends Paul, Anna and I went to visit one of the few remaining orange groves in Los Angeles' San Fernando Valley. Believe it or not, although I spent six years of my childhood in Florida, I never saw an orange grove. So, on this day in "the Valley," we went crazy climbing trees and grabbing bags of oranges. Fun activity, but at the end of the day we had about 50 oranges and nothing to do with them. That's how this cake was born.

1. Follow the recipe for the Lemon Pound Cake, except, in step #5, substitute 5 tbsp of orange zest for the lemon zest in the recipe and replace the lemon juice with 1/4 cup of fresh orange juice.

Chrysta's Recommended Finishing Touches:
Plain
Orange Glaze, page 141

Almond Pound Cake
For big ol' bundt pan only

I can remember being about six or seven, sitting in my dad's kitchen and showering the room with almond shells as I frantically cracked and pounded, trying to fill my tummy with my favorite nut. As an adult, I still love almonds but I've traded in the mess of shelling for the essence of almond captured in this cake. Ground almonds combined with pure almond extract flavor the batter and slivered almonds decorate the top, giving the cake layers of almond flavor. In my more sophisticated moments, I rather enjoy pairing this almond delight with black tea or coffee, accented by a little Amaretto di Saronno.

ingredients:

1 1/2 C unsalted butter

3 C sugar

5 eggs, room temperature

2 1/2 C flour

2 tsp baking powder

1/2 C ground almonds (or pre-ground almond meal)

1/4 tsp salt

2 tsp almond extract

1/2 tsp vanilla extract

2 C whole milk

1/3 C slivered almonds, enough to cover the bottom of pan (optional)

1. Preheat oven to 350 degrees.

2. Beat butter with an electric mixer on a medium-slow speed while slowly adding sugar. Continue until mixture is fluffy, about 3 minutes.

3. Crack eggs into a separate bowl and add to batter one at a time. Then beat on medium speed for an additional two minutes.

4. In another bowl, sift together flour, baking powder, and ground almonds and salt. Set aside.

5. Add the almond and vanilla extracts to the milk.

6. Turn the mixer speed to low. Beginning and ending with the flour, add 1/3 of the flour to the mixing bowl,

then 1/2 of the milk mixture, alternating until all ingredients are mixed.

7. Prepare pan with a coating of baker's cooking spray that includes flour (or greased and floured). Sprinkle the slivered almonds evenly around the bottom of the pan (optional), then pour batter into the pan.

8. Bake until just done, about 55 minutes or until inserted cake tester or skewer comes out clean—check cake often to be sure not to over bake.

9. Invert cake onto a cooling rack or serving plate. If cake resists, cool in the pan for 15 minutes before inverting. (If cake still resists, cool an additional 15 minutes in the pan.) Cool completely before glazing, at least 1 hour.

Chrysta's Recommended Finishing Touches:
Plain
Dusting of powdered sugar
Vanilla Glaze, page 139
Sliced with Fresh Strawberries
and a Dollop of Whipped Cream, page 144

7UP Pound Cake
For big ol' bundt pan only

I once heard—and later verified—a rumor that 7UP soda was initially marketed as a hangover cure. I've had a little experience with this cake and hangovers and I have to say, this is one food that can get me to rally. The cake is sweet, tangy and just melt-in-your-mouth good, thanks, in part, to the liberal use of 7UP glaze spooned over the hot cake. One slice of this cake (not that you can stop at one slice) and you'll start to feel better. Don't be surprised if you find yourself eating a third of this cake in one sitting.

ingredients:

2 tbsp lemon juice

2 tsp lime juice

1/2 tsp vanilla extract

1 C 7UP, (or other lemon-lime soda)*

1 1/2 C unsalted butter

3 C sugar

5 eggs, room temperature

zest of 3 large lemons

zest of 6 medium limes

3 C flour

1. Preheat oven to 350 degrees.

2. In a glass, add juices and vanilla extract to the 7UP. Set aside.

3. Beat butter with an electric mixer on a medium-slow speed while slowly adding sugar. Continue until mixture is fluffy, about 3 minutes.

4. Crack eggs into a separate bowl and add to batter one at a time. Then beat on medium speed for an additional 2 minutes.

5. Add zests.

6. Turn the mixer speed to low. Beginning and ending with the flour, add 1/3 of the flour to the mixing bowl, then 1/2 of the 7UP mixture, alternating until all ingredients are mixed. The batter will look slightly curdled. Don't worry, that's normal.

7. Pour batter into a big ol' bundt pan that has been coated with a baker's cooking spray that includes flour (or greased and floured).

8. Bake until just done, about 55 minutes or until inserted cake tester or skewer comes out clean— check cake often to be sure not to over bake.

9. While the cake is baking, make the 7UP glaze (see below).

10. When the cake is baked, cool in the pan for 10 minutes before inverting onto a plate. (If cake still resists, cool an additional 15 minutes in the pan.)

11. Pour 1/2 of the 7UP glaze on the cake while the cake is still hot. Some of the glaze will be absorbed and some will pool around the bottom of the plate.

12. Once the cake is cool, drizzle the remaining glaze over the top. In 15 minutes, or when the glaze has set, re-plate on a clean cake plate.

7UP Glaze

ingredients:

1/2 C 7UP, (or other lemon-lime soda)*

1 1/2 C powdered sugar

*To cut some of the sugar, you can substitute diet lemon-lime soda. The flavor of the cake will not quite have the same tangy bite as the original, but if you're watching your sugar, it's a great option.

1. Pour 7UP into a small mixing bowl.

2. With a whisk, add the powdered sugar 1/2 cup at a time until fully mixed.

Glaze 7UP Cake according to the baking instructions.

pound bundts   77

• 4 •

Chocolate Bundts

About two years ago I saw a television special on the origins of chocolate. It was a pivotal moment. That special and the subsequent research it inspired, drove me to change the chocolate cake recipe I'd been using for years—one that had been passed to me by my Aunt Dia, the master baker! Here, in a nutshell (or more appropriately, cacao shell), is how I learned to control the chocolate flavor and create addictively intense, moist chocolate cakes:

Chocolate comes from the seeds of the tropical cacao tree. When the seeds are fermented, dried and roasted, the shell is removed and the interior nibs are collected. These cocoa nibs are then processed into chocolate liquor. (No, you can't get drunk on chocolate liquor!) The two main components of chocolate liquor are cocoa powder and cocoa butter. Cocoa butter is the natural vegetable fat existing in chocolate liquor. Cocoa powder is made when almost all of the cocoa butter is removed from the chocolate liquor. Cocoa butter gives the cocoa powder a slick, almost wet feel.

Your average grocery store's cocoa powder contains about 7%-9% cocoa butter. But cocoa butter brings a satisfying intensity and moisture to chocolate cake. So, as I began to better understand the role of cocoa butter, I started experimenting with a high-fat, premium powder; one with about 22%-24% cocoa butter. This higher fat cocoa powder pretty much guarantees brilliantly rich and vibrant chocolate flavor without any extra effort.

The other change to my original recipe that that television special inspired was omitting melted chocolate from the recipe. To be honest, I always thought that the melted chocolate in my batter made the cake heavy. So I nixed the chocolate and concentrated on the proportion of my high-fat cocoa powder. (This not only gives me the desired texture and intensity, but also allows me to control the amount of sugar in the final batter.)

Now, when you go to bake a chocolate cake, it is important to understand that there are two types of unsweetened cocoa powder: "natural" and "Dutch-processed." Dutch-processed cocoa powder is treated (processed) to neutralize the cocoa's natural acid. You use Dutch-processed cocoa in cakes with acidic ingredients or ones using baking powder as the raising agent to ensure the proper cake consistency. Natural, unsweetened cocoa powder still has its acids. Typically, you use natural cocoa powder in recipes that call for baking soda, an ingredient that neutralizes the acids in the cocoa. However, the chocolate recipes in this book use baking powder and baking soda, so you can use either natural or Dutch-processed cocoa powder. The choice is yours.

*See page 148 for recommended brands and sources.

Basic Chocolate Cake

This cake is one of the best-selling items in my bakeshop and it is the foundation of many of Kiss My Bundt Bakery's cake variations. In this chapter, I provide you with a few of my variations. Soon, you'll see where you too can experiment. Once you get the hang of the basic cake, you might try swapping out vanilla for another natural extract or replace the boiling water with tea, coffee, or even use half-boiling water and half dark-rum.

At the bakery, we top this cake with everything from Oreo Buttercream to Cream Cheese Frosting. Sometimes, I like this cake plain and served with a glass of milk or a glass of red wine.

1. Preheat oven to 350 degrees.
2. Sift together sugar, flour, cocoa, baking soda, baking powder and salt in large bowl. Set aside.
3. Combine the eggs, milk, oil and vanilla. Using an electric mixer, beat on medium speed for 1 minute.
4. With the mixer on low speed, add dry ingredients to the wet, 1/2 cup at a time. Do this slowly so that the batter doesn't develop clumps.

ingredients:

1 3/4 C sugar

2 C all purpose flour

3/4 C high-fat cocoa powder*

1 1/4 tsp baking soda

1 1/4 tsp baking powder

3/4 tsp salt

2 eggs, room temperature

1 C of whole milk

1/2 C vegetable oil

2 tsp vanilla extract

1 C water, boiling

*See page 148 for recommended brands and sources

5. When thoroughly combined (do not overmix), slowly mix in boiling water. Note: the batter will be thin.

6. Transfer batter to cake pan(s) that have been coated with a baker's cooking spray that includes flour (or greased and floured), filling until cavity is about 3/4 full.

7. Bake cake(s) until an inserted toothpick or cake tester comes out clean—about 45 minutes for a big ol' bundt.

8. Invert cake(s) onto a cooling rack or serving plate. If cake resists, cool in the pan for 15 minutes before inverting. (If cake still resists, cool an additional 15 minutes in the pan.) Cool completely before frosting, at least 1 hour for a big ol' bundt.

Chrysta's Favorite Frostings & Finishing Touches:

Chocolate Buttercream, page127

Chocolate Ganache, page 143

Dark Chocolate Glaze, page 142

Coconut Buttercream
(it's like an Almond Joy), page 129

Cream Cheese Frosting, page 136

Mocha Buttercream, page 128

Oreo Buttercream, page 128

Vanilla Buttercream, page 127

Chocolate Sprinkles

Mint Chocolate Cake

Anyone who has ever had a Girl Scout in the family knows the Thin Mint. This cake is sort of an homage to that bestseller of my Girl Scout days. It tastes most like a Thin Mint when topped with Chocolate Glaze. But you can also serve it with vanilla ice cream, a glass of milk or a traditional Mint Julep.

additional ingredient:
1 tbsp pure peppermint extract

Reduce vanilla to 1 tsp.

1. Follow the recipe for basic chocolate cake, but, in step #3, reduce vanilla to 1 tsp and add 1 tbsp of pure peppermint extract.

Chrysta's Favorite Frostings & Finishing Touches:
Chocolate Buttercream, page 127
Dark Chocolate Glaze, page 142
Chocolate Ganache, page 143
Cream Cheese Frosting, page 136
Andes Candies (sliced in two on the diagonal)

Mandarin Chocolate Cake

I like to serve this cake with the simple Chocolate Glaze and a Riesling dessert wine, especially one with flavors that hint at orange.

additional ingredients:
zest of 2 medium oranges

1 tbsp pure orange extract, (or 1/2 tsp of pure orange oil)

Reduce vanilla to 1 tsp.

1. Follow the recipe for basic chocolate cake, but, in step #3, reduce vanilla to 1 tsp and add the orange zest and extract (or oil).

Chrysta's Favorite Frostings & Finishing Touches:
Chocolate Buttercream, page 127
Orange Buttercream, page 130
Dark Chocolate Glaze, page 142
Chocolate Ganache, page 143
Mandarin Segments

Molten Chocolate Minis

For chocoholics, nothing can improve on decadent chocolate cake...except maybe the addition of *more* chocolate. Dropping cold ganache into the batter of these mini bundts brings a surprise of melting chocolate oozing from the center of each cake. Serve straight from the oven for a molten chocolate delight.

1. Make the Chocolate Ganache recipe, below. Put in a heat safe bowl and cool in the refrigerator for 1 hour.

2. Make the Chocolate Cake batter according to the recipe on page 80.

3. Pour 2 tbsp of cake batter to pans that have been coated with a baker's cooking spray that includes flour, or greased and floured

4. Take 1 tbsp of cold chocolate ganache and, using rubber gloves, form the ganache into a football-shape.

*Recipe designed for mini bundt pans with no center cylinder or muffin tins only (for sources see page 150).

5. Drop the ganache ball into the middle of a mini bundt pan cavity.

6. Spoon 2 more tablespoons of chocolate batter into each mini bundt pan cavity. Note: the ganache ball will still be visible.

7. Bake in the oven for 18 minutes, or until a toothpick inserted into the side of the cake comes out clean. (If you stick the toothpick into the center of the cake, it will be wet from the ganache.)

8. Let baked cakes rest in the pan for 2 minutes. Turn the cakes out onto a cooling rack.

9. Serve immediately as is, or dust with powdered sugar.

ingredients:

3 oz (about 1/2 C) bitter-sweet 60%-70% chocolate chips or grated chocolate*

1/4 C and 2 tbsp heavy cream

*See page 148 for recommended brands and sources.

for the ganache

1. In a saucepan, whisk cream over medium-high heat.

2. Bring to a near boil, (about 190 degrees if you have a thermometer). You do not want the cream to boil but it should be hot enough to melt the chocolate.

3. Remove from heat and stir in chocolate.

4. Whisk the chocolate into the cream until it has melted.

Mocha Cake

Whoever discovered the perfect partners of coffee and chocolate should have their own public holiday. Just like the popular espresso shop drink, this cake celebrates the depth and richness of the pairing. Topped with chocolate buttercream, this cake is my favorite companion to a cup of joe, served black, no sugar.

1. Preheat oven to 350 degrees.

2. Sift together sugar, flour, cocoa, baking soda, baking powder and salt in large bowl. Set aside.

3. Combine the eggs, milk, oil, and vanilla. Using an electric mixer, beat on medium speed 1 minute.

ingredients:

- 1 3/4 C sugar
- 2 C all purpose flour
- 3/4 C high-fat cocoa powder*
- 1 1/4 tsp baking soda
- 1 1/4 tsp baking powder
- 3/4 tsp salt
- 2 eggs, room temperature
- 1 C whole milk
- 1/2 C vegetable oil
- 2 tsp vanilla extract
- 1 C drip coffee, brought to a boil
- 5 tbsp instant coffee granules

*See page 148 for recommended brands and sources.

4. With the mixer on low, add dry ingredients to the wet, 1/2 cup at a time. Do this slowly so that the batter doesn't develop clumps.

5. Bring drip coffee to a boil and stir in the instant coffee granules.

6. When batter is thoroughly combined (do not overmix), slowly mix in boiling coffee. Note: the batter will be thin.

7. Transfer batter to cake pan(s) that have been coated with a baker's cooking spray that includes flour (or greased and floured), filling until cavity is about 3/4 full.

8. Bake cake(s) until an inserted toothpick or cake tester comes out clean—about 45 minutes for a big ol' bundt.

9. Invert cake(s) onto a cooling rack or serving plate. If cake resists, cool in the pan for 15 minutes before inverting. (If cake still resists, cool an additional 15 minutes in the pan.) Cool completely before frosting, at least 1 hour for a big ol' bundt.

Chrysta's Favorite Frostings & Finishing Touches:

Mocha Buttercream, page 128
Chocolate Ganache, page 143
Dark Chocolate Glaze, page 142
Vanilla Buttercream, page 127
Cream Cheese Frosting, page 136
Chocolate Covered Espresso Beans

Irish Coffee Cake

I've learned my way around an Irish pub or two and have had plenty of personal experience with Irish Coffee. This cake is a baker's riff on that legendary drink.

1. Preheat oven to 350 degrees.

2. Sift together sugar, flour, cocoa, baking soda, baking powder and salt in large bowl. Set aside.

3. Combine the eggs, milk, oil and vanilla. Using an electric mixer, beat on medium speed for 1 minute.

4. Add dry ingredients to the wet, 1/2 cup at a time. Do this slowly so that the batter doesn't develop clumps.

5. Bring drip coffee to a boil and stir in the instant coffee granules. Stir in the whiskey.

6. When batter is thoroughly combined (do not overmix), slowly mix in boiling coffee mixture. Note: the batter will be thin.

7. Transfer batter to cake pan(s) that have been coated with a baker's cooking spray that includes flour (or greased and floured), filling until cavity is about 3/4 full.

8. Bake cake(s) until an inserted toothpick or cake tester comes out clean—about 45 minutes for a big ol' bundt.

ingredients:

1 3/4 C sugar

2 C all purpose flour

3/4 C high-fat cocoa powder*

1 1/4 tsp baking soda

1 1/4 tsp baking powder

3/4 tsp salt

2 eggs, room temperature

1 C of whole milk

1/2 C vegetable oil

2 tsp vanilla extract

1/2 C drip coffee, boiling

1/2 C Irish whiskey (such as Jamesons)

5 tbsp instant coffee granules

*See page 148 for recommended brands and sources.

9. Invert cake(s) onto a cooling rack or serving plate. If cake resists, cool in the pan for 15 minutes before inverting. (If cake still resists, cool an additional 15 minutes in the pan.) Cool completely before frosting, at least 1 hour for a big ol' bundt.

Chrysta's Favorite Frostings & Finishing Touches:
Cream Cheese Frosting, page 136
Vanilla Buttercream, page 127

Mexican *Hot* Chocolate Cake

The Aztecs invented a drink of hot chocolate accented with chile pepper, vanilla and other spices over 600 years ago. The drink was believed to create a sense of well-being. My cake is based on the Aztec super-drink. It is intended to offer the same effects as the original.

1. Preheat oven to 350 degrees.
2. Sift together sugar, flour, cocoa, baking soda, baking powder, cinnamon, cayenne and salt in large bowl. Set aside.

ingredients:

1 3/4 C sugar

2 C flour

3/4 C high-fat cocoa powder*

1 1/4 tsp baking soda

1 1/4 tsp baking powder

1 1/2 tbsp ground cinnamon

1 1/2 tsp ground cayenne pepper

3/4 tsp salt

2 eggs, room temperature

1 C whole milk

1/2 C vegetable oil

2 tsp vanilla extract

1 C boiling water**

*See page 142 for recommended brands and sources.

**For added richness, you can swap out the water for 1 cup of boiling drip coffee.

3. Combine eggs, milk, oil, and vanilla. Using an electric mixer, beat on medium speed for 1 minute.

4. With the mixer on low speed, add dry ingredients to the wet, 1/2 cup at a time. Do this slowly so that the batter doesn't develop clumps.

5. When thoroughly combined (do not over mix) slowly mix in boiling water. Note: the batter will be thin.

6. Transfer batter to cake pan(s) that have been coated with a baker's cooking spray that includes flour (or greased and floured), filling until cavity is about 3/4 full.

7. Bake cake(s) until an inserted toothpick or cake tester comes out clean—about 45 minutes for a big ol' bundt.

8. Invert cake(s) onto a cooling rack or serving plate. If cake resists, cool in the pan for 15 minutes before inverting. (If cake still resists, cool an additional 15 minutes in the pan.) Cool completely before frosting, at least 1 hour for a big ol' bundt.

Chrysta's Favorite Frostings & Finishing Touches:
Chocolate Buttercream, page 127
Chocolate Ganache, page 143
Dark Chocolate Glaze, page 142

Cabernet Chocolate Cake with Blackberry Red Wine Glaze

Inspired by my friend, Amy Reiley, an aphrodisiac expert (and editor of this book), this cake pairs the two aphrodisiacs of chocolate and wine. Layered with flavor, the cake is first glazed with a red wine glaze, then drizzled with chocolate glaze or ganache. Served with a glass of Cabernet Sauvignon, the arousing combination is sure to at least get some fingers or lips licked.

1. Preheat oven to 350 degrees.

2. Sift together sugar, flour, cocoa, baking soda, baking powder and salt in large bowl. Set aside.

3. Combine the eggs, milk, oil and vanilla. Using an electric mixer beat on medium speed for 1 minute.

4. With the mixer on low speed, add dry ingredients to the wet, 1/2 cup at a time. Do this slowly so that the batter doesn't develop clumps. (Do not over mix)

5. Combine the water and wine and bring to a boil.

6. When the batter is thoroughly combined (do not overmix), slowly mix in boiling water and wine mixture. Note: the batter will be thin.

7. Transfer batter to cake pan(s) that have been coated with a baker's cooking spray that includes flour (or greased and floured), filling until cavity is about 3/4 full.

ingredients:

1 3/4 C sugar

2 C flour

3/4 C high-fat cocoa powder*

1 1/4 tsp baking soda

1 1/4 tsp baking powder

1/2 tsp salt

2 eggs, room temperature

1 C whole milk

1/2 C vegetable oil

2 tsp vanilla extract

1/2 C water

1/2 C of Cabernet Sauvignon, (or other dry red wine)

*See page 148 for recommended brands and sources.

8. Bake cake(s) until an inserted toothpick or cake tester comes out clean—about 45 minutes for a big ol' bundt.

9. Invert cake(s) onto a cooling rack or serving plate. If cake resists, cool in the pan for 15 minutes before inverting. (If cake still resists, cool an additional 15 minutes in the pan.) Cool completely before frosting, at least 1 hour for a big ol' bundt.

10. Drizzle blackberry glaze, (below), over the cooled chocolate cake.

11. Pour warm chocolate ganache (143) or chocolate glaze (142) over the red wine-glazed cake.

Blackberry Red Wine Glaze

ingredients:

4 tbsp seedless blackberry fruit spread or pre-serves

1/3 C Cabernet Sauvignon, (or other dry red wine)

1. In a small saucepan, whisk wine and blackberry preserves over medium heat.

2. Once incorporated, bring mixture to a boil and boil for 1 minute, (this helps thicken the glaze).

3. Remove from heat and let mixture cool for 3 minutes.

4. Spoon over chocolate cake. The amount is up to your preference, but I use 1 tbsp each for mini bundts, 2 tbsp each for a baby bundts and the entire batch of glaze over a big ol' bundt.

Chocolate Bacon Cake

Many of my best childhood memories are studded with bacon. The thought of pancakes with syrup and bacon still makes my mouth water. That childhood breakfast combo taught me the great culinary secret: salty and sweet make incredible partners. This chocolate bacon cake takes the paring to the next level by partnering smoky bacon with sweet, dark-chocolate goodness.

for the bacon

1. Preheat the oven to 350 degrees.

2. Cut bacon strips into bite-sized pieces. Cook over medium heat until the bacon is browned and crisp. (You can also cook bacon in the oven on a shallow baking dish lined with foil. Cook at 350 degrees, stirring occasionally, until bacon is brown.)

3. Scoop bacon out of your frying pan and place in a mesh colander/strainer. Press the bacon with the back of a spoon to remove extra grease. Take strained grease plus the grease in your pan and measure. This 1 lb of bacon should yield about 1/2 cup of bacon grease. Set grease aside. If you are short on grease, supplement the difference with vegetable oil.

4. To make the bacon sprinkles, spread the drained, chopped bacon pieces on a parchment-lined cookie sheet. Cover with the 1/3 cup brown sugar.

ingredients:

1 lb plain or lightly-smoked, thin-cut bacon*

1/3 C brown sugar

1 3/4 C granulated sugar

2 C flour

3/4 C high-fat cocoa powder*

1 1/4 tsp baking soda

1 1/4 tsp baking powder

1/2 tsp salt

2 eggs, room temperature

1 C whole milk

2 tsp vanilla extract

1/2 C bacon grease, (from the 1 lb of bacon)

1 C boiling water

*Heavily-smoked bacon can impart the smoke flavor on the cake. I use applewood smoked, which just lends a hint of its flavor to the cake.

*See page 148 for recommended brands and sources.

5. Bake in the oven for 12-15 minutes, checking occasionally. The bacon will get crisp in the oven as the brown sugar sweetens it and the grease pulls away.

6. Sort out the bacon pieces from the brown sugar.

7. Finely chop the bacon pieces by hand until you have bacon sprinkles. Add this to the cake in step 8.

8. Save the remaining bacon sprinkles in an air-tight container. Use within a week. You can use as bacon sprinkles on top of a cake frosted with buttercream.

for the cake

1. Preheat oven to 350 degrees.

2. Sift together sugar, flour, cocoa, baking powder, baking soda and salt in large bowl. Set aside.

3. Put eggs, milk, bacon grease and vanilla into a mixing bowl. Using an electric mixer beat on medium speed for 1 minute.

4. Add dry ingredients to the beaten egg mixture, 1/2 cup at a time. Do this slowly so that the batter doesn't develop clumps.

5. Once the batter is well mixed, slowly add boiling water. Note: the batter will be thin.

6. Fold in 1/3 cup of bacon sprinkles. (See bacon recipe above.)

7. Transfer batter to cake pan(s) that have been coated with a baker's cooking spray that includes flour (or greased and floured), filling until cavity is about 3/4 full.

8. Bake cake(s) until an inserted toothpick or cake tester comes out clean—about 45 minutes for a big ol' bundt.

9. Invert cake(s) onto a cooling rack or serving plate. If cake resists, cool in the pan for 15 minutes before inverting. (If cake still resists, cool an additional 15 minutes in the pan.) Cool completely before frosting, at least 1 hour for a big ol' bundt.

Chrysta's Favorite Frostings & Finishing Touches:
Chocolate Buttercream, page 127
Chocolate Ganache, page 143
Bacon Sprinkles

vanilla birthday
cake with vanilla
buttercream and
multi-colored
sanding sugar

cinnamon pecan coffee cake

almond pound cake

opposite page

top left: chocolate cake with chocolate ganache

top right: molten chocolate mini

bottom: red velvet mini bundts

chocolate bacon cake with
bacon sprinkles

champagne minis with champagne buttercream

from left to right: almond cake; baby irish coffee cake; mini red velvet, mandarin chocolate, strawberry lemonade and vegan chocolate bliss cake (on stand); coconut cake with coconut frosting; chocolate peanut butter marble cake; pineapple upside down cake; chocolate mint cake with chocolate glaze; and baby chocolate, vanilla and strawberry cakes (on stand)

tools of the trade: *(clockwise)* big ol' bundt, stand mixer, all-purpose flour, baby bundt pans, spatula, crank-style sifter, mini bundt pans, whisk, zester, measuring cup, measuring spoons

left: marbling the batter for a chocolate and vanilla marble cake

above: zesting citrus with a microplane zester

right: mac 'n cheese baby bundt
below: raspberry lemonade picnic cake

mexican *hot* chocolate cake

• 5 •

Other Bundts

Beyond vanilla, chocolate and pound cakes, we sell several popular cakes at the bakery that don't fit into any of the standard categories. What they have in common is that they are all particularly moist—and they are among Kiss My Bundt's most popular cakes. Several of the bundts in this chapter have an ingredient that brings a level of moisture beyond what the butter or oil brings to a cake, such as pumpkin purée, brown sugar or buttermilk. They are all very different from my vanilla-based and chocolate cakes but so good they had to have a section in the book. Do not let the title of this chapter fool you. "Other" does not mean leftovers. I like to think of these as the cakes that are so good, so interesting, that they are of another world!

Chrysta's Carrot Cake

As a little girl, I loved carrot cake—except for the chunks of the pineapple and raisins Southerners insist on piling into their carrot cake, which I in turn painstakingly poked out before I could enjoy my slice. Cake with lumps of warm fruit is a texture with which I take issue even today. I once asked my Aunt Dia why the extra fruit goes in the cake. She replied that pineapple and raisins add moisture to carrot cake. Hello? Carrots have moisture! At the bakery, I make my carrot cake with walnuts, not fruit. But it is most definitely moist enough to make Aunt Dia proud. I think this cake is perfect unadorned, but try it with cold cream cheese frosting for a new taste sensation.

ingredients:

2 C flour

3/4 tsp salt

1 1/2 tbsp cinnamon

1 1/2 tsp baking soda

1 1/4 C vegetable oil

1 1/2 C white granulated
sugar

1/4 C brown sugar,
packed

4 eggs, room temperature

3 C carrots, grated

3/4 C walnuts, finely
chopped

1. Preheat oven to 350 degrees.

2. Sift flour, salt, cinnamon and baking soda together.

3. Using an electric mixer, blend oil and sugars, mixing for 1 minute.

4. Crack eggs into a separate bowl and add to batter one at a time. Then beat on medium speed for an additional 2 minutes.

5. Slowly add the flour mixture 1/2 cup at a time. Batter will be thick.

6. Fold in grated carrots and walnuts. Stir by hand until fully incorporated.

7. Transfer batter to cake pans that have been coated with a baker's cooking spray that includes flour (or greased and floured), filling until cavities are about 3/4 full.

8. Bake cake(s) until an inserted toothpick or cake tester comes out clean—about 40 minutes for a big ol' bundt.

9. Invert cake(s) onto a cooling rack or serving plate. If cake resists, cool in the pan for 15 minutes before inverting. (If cake still resists, cool an additional 15 minutes in the pan.) Cool completely before frosting, at least 1 hour for a big ol' bundt.

Chrysta's Favorite Frostings & Finishing Touches:
Plain
Cream Cheese Frosting, page 136

Harvest Pumpkin Cake

My best friend from high school, Anagha, loves anything pumpkin. Once I visited her when she was in law school and in honor of the occasion, we tried to incorporate pumpkin into every meal: pumpkin pancakes, ice cream, ravioli, even pumpkin beer! But we never found any pumpkin cake. So I developed this cake for her. The newest tradition is a slice of pumpkin cake with a cold pumpkin beer. Trust me, it works.

1. Preheat oven to 350 degrees.

2. Sift together flour, baking powder, baking soda, pumpkin pie spice and salt. Set aside.

3. Using an electric mixer, beat eggs on medium speed until frothy, 3-4 minutes.

4. Turn mixer speed to low and slowly add sugars. Beat until very thick.

5. At a medium speed, mix in pumpkin purée and oil, mixing until thoroughly incorporated.

6. With the mixer on low, add dry ingredients to the wet 1/2 cup at a time. Do this slowly so that the batter doesn't develop clumps.

7. Transfer batter to cake pans that have been coated with a baker's cooking spray that includes flour (or greased and floured), filling until cavities are about 3/4 full.

ingredients

3 C flour

1 tbsp baking powder

1 tbsp baking soda

1 tbsp pumpkin pie spice

1 tsp salt

4 eggs, room temperature

1 C granulated sugar

1 C brown sugar, packed

15-16 oz can pumpkin purée, (not pumpkin pie filling)

1 C vegetable oil

8. Bake cake(s) until an inserted toothpick or cake tester comes out clean—about 40 minutes for a big ol' bundt.

9. Invert cake(s) onto a cooling rack or serving plate. If cake resists, cool in the pan for 15 minutes before inverting. (If cake still resists, cool an additional 15 minutes in the pan.) Cool completely before frosting, at least 1 hour for a big ol' bundt.

Chrysta's Favorite Frostings & Finishing Touches:
Cream Cheese Frosting, page 136
Cinnamon Glaze, page 139

Peanut Butter Lover's Cake

My sister Jamille *loves* peanut butter. From childhood days, those peanut butter cookies with the fork imprint (or topped with a Reese's Peanut Butter Cup for a real treat) have always topped her list. I created this peanut butter cake as something she might like but my customers ended up loving it, too. Topped with chocolate buttercream or chocolate glaze, a cold glass of milk on the side, it puts Mr. Reeses to shame.

1. Preheat oven to 350 degrees.

2. Sift together flour and baking powder. Set aside.

3. Using an electric mixer, beat peanut butter, butter and sugars on a medium low speed until blended.

4. Add oil and continue to beat to incorporate.

5. Increase speed medium high and beat mixture until fluffy, about 3 minutes.

6. Reduce speed to low and add eggs one at a time, then beat on medium for an additional 2 minutes.

7. Add vanilla.

ingredients

2 C flour

2 tsp baking powder

3/4 C smooth peanut butter, (chunky is not recommended)

3/4 C unsalted butter

1 C granulated sugar

1/2 C brown sugar

1/3 C vegetable oil

2 eggs, room temperature

2 tsp vanilla

2/3 C milk

8. Beginning and ending with the flour, mix 1/3 of the flour, then 1/2 of the milk, alternating, with the mixer on low, until all ingredients are mixed.

7. Transfer batter to cake pans that have been coated with a baker's cooking spray that includes flour (or greased and floured), filling until cavities are about 3/4 full.

8. Bake cake(s) until an inserted toothpick or cake tester comes out clean—about 40 minutes for a big ol' bundt.

9. Invert cake(s) onto a cooling rack or serving plate. If cake resists, cool in the pan for 15 minutes before inverting. (If cake still resists, cool an additional 15 minutes in the pan.) Cool completely before frosting, at least 1 hour for a big ol' bundt.

Chrysta's Favorite Frostings & Finishing Touches:

Chocolate Buttercream, page 127
Chocolate Glaze, page 142
Vanilla Buttercream, page 127
Cream Cheese Frosting, page 136
Chocolate Sprinkles

Cinnamon Pecan Coffee Cake

This recipe is basically a super-moist breakfast cake. The ribbon of cinnamon and pecans add sweetness and additional moisture to the cake's slightly tart, sour cream flavor. With the brown sugar in the swirl, the cake is plenty sweet on its own but I like to add the decadence of cinnamon sugar glaze.

1. Preheat oven to 350 degrees.

2. Stir vanilla, milk, sour cream together. Set aside.

3. In a small bowl mix the swirl ingredients, (see recipe below). Set aside.

4. Sift flour and baking powder and salt together. Set aside.

5. Using an electric mixer, beat butter on a medium-low speed while slowly adding the sugars. Continue to beat until mixture is fluffy, about 3 minutes.

6. Crack eggs into a separate bowl and add to batter one at a time. Then beat on medium speed for an additional 2 minutes.

7. Beginning and ending with the flour, add 1/3 of the flour into the wet mixture followed by 1/2 of the milk and sour cream mixture, alternating until all ingredients are mixed.

9. Pour 1/3 of the batter into a big ol' bundt pan that has been coated with a baker's cooking spray that includes flour, (or greased and floured).*

ingredients:
2 tsp vanilla extract
1/4 C whole milk
1 3/4 C sour cream
3 C flour
1 tsp baking soda
2 tsp baking powder
3/4 teaspoon salt
3/4 C unsalted butter
1 C sugar
1/2 C brown sugar, packed
3 eggs, room temperature

for the swirl
3/4 C pecans, finely chopped
1 1/2 C packed brown sugar
3 tbsp cinnamon

10. Sprinkle 1/2 of the swirl on top of the batter. Add an additional 1/3 of the batter and repeat adding swirl. Top with remaining batter.

11. Bake until an inserted toothpick or cake tester comes out clean, about 55 minutes for a big ol' bundt. (The swirl becomes wet during the baking, so be sure to stick your tester into the batter not the swirl.)

12. Invert cake(s) onto a cooling rack or serving plate. If cake resists, cool in the pan for 15 minutes before inverting. (If cake still resists, cool an additional 15 minutes in the pan.) Cool completely before glazing, at least 1 hour for a big ol' bundt.

* For making baby, mini bundts or cupcakes, fill greased and floured pans 1/2 full with batter. Top with 1 tbsp of swirl for a mini bundt or 2 1/2 tbsp of swirl for a baby bundt. Then fill the cavity to 3/4 with additional batter before baking.

Chrysta's Favorite Frostings & Finishing Touches:
Plain
Cinnamon Sugar Glaze, page 139
Vanilla Glaze, page 139

Red Velvet Cake

Red Velvet is without a doubt the best selling cake at Kiss My Bundt Bakery. I've had customers wait over an hour in the shop for a fresh batch when we've sold out. Though nobody hesitates to order it, I still get the constant question, "What IS Red Velvet?" Some bakers merely add red dye to their vanilla or chocolate cakes and call it Red Velvet. This is not Red Velvet! Red Velvet should be a light cocoa cake but it shouldn't taste overwhelmingly chocolaty. Made correctly, it possesses a hint of sourness and a moist, dense texture that, especially when topped with cream cheese frosting, is at once one of the most comforting and simply "cake-like" of my cakes and, paradoxically, one of the most complex.

1. Preheat oven to 350 degrees.

2. Using an electric mixer, combine oil, buttermilk, eggs, food coloring, vinegar and vanilla. Beat on medium speed for 1 minute.

3. In a separate bowl, sift together flour, sugar, baking soda, salt and cocoa powder.

4. With the mixer on low, add dry ingredients to the wet 1/2 cup at a time. Do this slowly so that the batter doesn't develop clumps.

5. Transfer batter to cake pans that have been coated with a baker's cooking spray that includes flour (or greased and floured), filling until cavities are about 3/4 full.

ingredients:

1 1/4 C vegetable oil

1 C buttermilk

2 eggs, room temperature

2 tbsp red food coloring*

1 tsp distilled white vinegar

1 tsp vanilla

2 1/2 C flour

1 3/4 C sugar

1 tsp baking soda

3/4 tsp fine salt

1 tbsp high-fat cocoa powder**

*To make a Brown Velvet, omit red food coloring from recipe (see additional notes in Vegan Brown Velvet, 112).

**See for recommended brands and suppliers, 148.

6. Bake cake(s) until an inserted toothpick or cake tester comes out clean—about 40 minutes for a big ol' bundt.

7. Invert cake(s) onto a cooling rack or serving plate. If cake resists, cool in the pan for 15 minutes before inverting. (If cake still resists, cool an additional 15 minutes in the pan.) Cool completely before frosting, at least 1 hour for a big ol' bundt.

Chrysta's Favorite Frostings & Finishing Touches:
Cream Cheese Frosting, page 136

Vegan Cakes

When I was getting ready to open the bakery, one of my closest friends told me he wouldn't speak to me again unless I put a vegan option on my menu for him (one that doesn't include eggs or dairy and only uses brands of sugar made with vegan-friendly processing). It wasn't that challenging to produce a cake that could be labeled vegan. But what I wanted was a great cake that just happened to be vegan. After much trial and error, I am very proud to have a cake that gets the comment, "This is good. It's Vegan?" Not "It's good...for Vegan."

Vegan Red Velvet was the cake I created for the bakery, basing it off of our best-seller. For this book, I also added Vegan Chocolate to my repertoire along with a few chocolate variations, to give the vegan at home a few more creative options. Oh, and the aforementioned friend not only still speaks to me but nowadays he eats a lot of cake!

Vegan Chocolate Bliss Cake

One of my newest creations, vegan chocolate cake is one of my easiest and most satisfying recipes. People are often surprised to learn it is vegan. Because this cake is moister than most, grease your pans extra generously to ensure it doesn't stick.

1. Preheat oven to 350 degrees.

2. Sift together sugar, flour, cocoa powder, baking powder, baking soda and salt. Set aside.

3. Add soymilk, oil and vanilla to a mixing bowl. Using an electric mixer, beat on medium speed for 1 minute.

4. With the mixer on low speed, add dry ingredients to the wet, 1/2 cup at a time. Do this slowly so that the batter doesn't develop clumps.

5. When thoroughly combined (do not overmix), slowly mix in boiling water. Note: the batter will be thin.

6. Transfer batter to cake pans that have been coated with a baker's cooking spray that includes flour (or greased and floured), filling until cavities are about 3/4 full.

ingredients:

1 3/4 C vegan sugar

2 C unbleached, organic all purpose flour

3/4 C high-fat cocoa powder*

1 1/4 tsp baking powder

1 1/4 tsp baking soda

3/4 tsp salt

1 C unsweetened soymilk

1/3 C vegetable oil

2 tsp vanilla extract

3/4 C water, boiling

*See page 148 for recommended brands and suppliers.

7. Bake cake(s) until an inserted toothpick or cake tester comes out clean—about 40 minutes for a big ol' bundt.

8. Invert cake(s) onto a cooling rack or serving plate. If cake resists, cool in the pan for 15 minutes before inverting. (If cake still resists, cool an additional 15 minutes in the pan.) Cool completely before frosting, at least 1 hour for a big ol' bundt.

Chrysta's Favorite Frostings & Finishing Touches:
Vegan Cream Cheese Frosting, page 138
Vegan Vanilla Frosting, page 135
Vegan Chocolate Frosting, page 135

Vegan Chocolate Cake Variations

You can easily turn your Vegan Chocolate Cake into a Vegan Mint Cake or Vegan Mandarin Chocolate cake.

For Mint, reduce the vanilla to 1 tsp and add 1 tbsp of pure peppermint extract to the batter. To make Mandarin, you should also just follow the Vegan Chocolate Bliss recipe, but add the zest of two oranges and 1 tbsp of pure orange extract, again reducing the vanilla to 1 tsp.

Vegan Mocha Cake

Follow the recipe for Vegan Chocolate Bliss but in step #5, bring the drip coffee to a boil and stir in instant coffee to dissolve before adding the boiling liquid to the cake batter.

additional ingredients:
5 tbsp instant coffee granules
3/4 C coffee, boiling

Chrysta's Favorite Frostings & Finishing Touches:
Vegan Vanilla Buttercream, page 135
Vegan Chocolate Buttercream, page 135

*Replace boiling water with the boiling drip coffee.

Vegan Red Velvet Cake

Although I'm a butter, eggs and even bacon girl, this cake has been very successful for me in Southern California (where it seems almost chic to have some sort of dietary restriction). If you are not vegan but want to cook for someone who is, make sure to shop for a sugar that is labeled vegan. Most brands of sugar have been processed with bone char (used to give the sugar its snow white color). Relying on the sugar stocked in your pantry may negate your hard work!

1. Preheat oven to 350 degrees.

2. Add vinegar to soymilk. Set aside for 10 minutes, allowing the mixture to curdle.

3. Sift together sugar, flour, baking soda, salt and cocoa powder.

ingredients:

- 1 tsp distilled white vinegar
- 1 C unsweetened soymilk
- 1 3/4 C vegan sugar
- 2 1/2 C unbleached, organic all purpose flour
- 1 tsp baking soda
- 3/4 tsp fine salt
- 1 tbsp high-fat cocoa powder*
- 1 C vegetable oil
- 2 tsp natural red food coloring, (omit altogether for a Brown Velvet cake)
- 1 tsp vanilla
- 1 C boiling water

*See page 148 for recommended brands and suppliers.

4. Add soymilk, oil, food coloring and vanilla to a mixing bowl. Using an electric mixer, beat on medium speed for 1 minute.

5. With the mixer on low speed, add dry ingredients to the wet, 1/2 cup at a time. Do this slowly so that the batter doesn't develop clumps.

6. When thoroughly combined (do not overmix), slowly mix in boiling water. Note: the batter will be thin.

7. Transfer batter to cake pans that have been coated with a baker's cooking spray that includes flour (or greased and floured), filling until cavities are about 3/4 full.

8. Bake cake(s) until an inserted toothpick or cake tester comes out clean—about 40 minutes for a big ol' bundt.

9. Invert cake(s) onto a cooling rack or serving plate. If cake resists, cool in the pan for 15 minutes before inverting. (If cake still resists, cool an additional 15 minutes in the pan.) Cool completely before frosting, at least 1 hour for a big ol' bundt.

Chrysta's Favorite Frostings & Finishing Touches:
Dusting of Vegan Powdered Sugar
Vegan Cream Cheese Frosting, page138

Vegan Brown Velvet Cake

In addition to vegans, in Southern California I meet many purists who prefer to avoid dyes, even natural ones, in their food. For these customers, I make Brown Velvet (aka Red Velvet left au naturel, colored only by the touch of cocoa powder added to the batter). To make this equally-delicious version, simply omit the red dye from the Vegan Red Velvet batter.

• 6 •

Marble Bundts

Marble cakes, those complex constructions with the graceful arcs and swirls of color, are simply mixtures of two or three different cake batters. These creative and richly-layered cakes just may be my favorite style of bundts.

I tend to be a bit indecisive, especially when faced with a difficult choice, such as which from a dozen flavors of cake should I choose. Marble cake allows me the decadence of more than one flavor in a single slice. And I love marble cake for its kaleidoscope patterns and colors. When I became a professional baker, what I grew to love most about marble is that it gives me something to do with the leftover cake batter.

You can use your batters at home in this way, too. Say for example, you made the Basic Vanilla Birthday Cake recipe but only needed one pan of mini bundts. You would still have about two cups of batter left. So, rather than make additional minis that you don't need or—heaven forbid—throw the batter away, you make marble cake!

Leftover batter from any cake in this book can be used for a marble. Batters typically will keep, refrigerated, for three days. Some of the best-selling marble cakes at my bakery are: Vanilla Chocolate, Marble, Peanut Butter, Chocolate Marble, and Banana Chocolate Marble.

But your marbling need only be limited by your imagination—at the bakery, we've even done Strawberry Banana and Chocolate Red Velvet marble cakes.

In case you don't happen to have leftover batter but still want to try your hand at these artful cakes, here are some half-batch quantities of recipes from earlier chapters perfect for combining to make a full-size (big ol' bundt) cake. Pick any two and follow the marbling tips below.

How to Marble

1. Coat your cake pan(s) with a baking spray that contains flour (or grease and flour).

2. Take the first batter and scoop a layer into the bottom of the pan.

3. Take the second batter and scoop a layer on top of the first batter.

4. Take a butter knife or coffee stirrer and begin to make a zig-zag or circular motion, swirling the batters to create ribbons of the bottom batter in the top batter. There isn't a "right" or "wrong" way to swirl your batters. It is abstract art.

5. Repeat steps 2 and 3 until your pan is filled 2/3 to 3/4 full.

Vanilla Cake

1 1/4 C flour

1 1/4 tsp baking powder

1/4 tsp salt

3 oz unsalted butter

3/4 C + 3tbsp sugar

2 eggs, room temperature

3/4 tsp vanilla

1/2 C whole milk

Follow recipe on page 28.

Banana Cake

1 1/4 tsp baking powder

1/4 tsp salt

1 1/4 C flour

3 oz unsalted butter

3/4 C + 3tbsp sugar

2 eggs, room temperature

1/2 C whole milk

3/4 tsp vanilla

1/2 mashed ripe banana

Follow recipe on page 34.

Chocolate Cake

3/4 C + 3tbsp sugar

1 C flour

1/2 C high-fat cocoa powder

1/2 tsp baking soda

1/2 tsp baking powder

1/2 tsp salt

1 large egg, room
temperature

1/2 C whole milk

1/4 C vegetable oil

1 tsp vanilla extract

1/2 C boiling water

Follow recipe on page 80.

Peanut Butter Cake

1 C flour

1 tsp baking powder

1/3 C smooth peanut butter

1/3 C unsalted butter

1/4 C vegetable oil

1/2 C granulated sugar

1/4 C brown sugar

1 egg, room temperature

1 tsp vanilla

1/3 C whole milk

Follow recipe on page 102.

Mocha Cake

3/4 C + 3tbsp sugar

1 C flour

1/2 C high-fat cocoa powder

1/2 tsp baking soda

1/2 tsp baking powder

1/2 tsp salt

1 large egg, room temperature

1/2 C whole milk

1/4 C vegetable oil

1 tsp vanilla extract

1/2 C drip coffee, boiling

3 tbsp instant coffee granules

Follow recipe on page 86.

Coconut Cake

1 1/4 C flour

1 1/4 tsp baking powder

1/4 tsp salt

3 oz unsalted butter

3/4 C + 3tbsp sugar

2 eggs, room temperature

3/4 tsp vanilla

1/2 C coconut milk

Follow recipe on page 32.

• 7 •
Savory Bundts

When you get hooked on bundt, you want to start cooking everything in the pretty, fluted-edge pan. Here are just a few of the variations I've moved from my casserole dish to my bundt pans. You can make any of these recipes in a casserole but try them in bundt pans and you'll understand why bundt reigns supreme in my kitchen.

Sweet Cornbread with Honey Butter

To set this cake apart from your average corn meal-based bread, I've gone a little sweet. (I am a cake baker, after all!) And to sweeten things even more, I've added a sinful topping. As you may have noticed by now, I love butter. What I love even more is butter mixed with honey. Serve this bread hot, straight out of the pan and slathered with honey butter and you'll understand why sweet cornbread is one of my favorite things.

1. Preheat oven to 350.

2. Sift flour, baking soda, baking powder and salt together. Stir in cornmeal and set aside.

3. Using an electric mixer on a medium-low speed, combine soft butter and sugar. Mix for 30 seconds, or until incorporated.

4. Mix in eggs one at a time until well blended. Wait 30 seconds between the addition of each egg.

5. Add buttermilk and mix until incorporated.

6. With mixer on a low speed, slowly add dry ingredients until well blended and relatively lump free. Note: batter will be thick.

7. Transfer batter to cake pans that have been coated with a baker's cooking spray that includes flour (or greased and floured), filling until cavities are about 3/4 full.

8. Bake cornbread(s) until an inserted toothpick, (or skewer for a big ol' bundt), comes out clean—about 40 minutes for a big ol' bundt.

9. Invert on a plate and serve warm. If cornbread resists, cool in pan for 15 minutes, then invert.

ingredients:

2 C flour

1 tsp baking soda

1 tsp baking powder

2 C cornmeal

1 C unsalted butter, softened

1 1/4 C sugar

4 eggs, room temperature

2 C buttermilk

1 1/2 tsp salt

for the honey butter

You can use salted or unsalted butter for this recipe, based on your personal preference. Some like the sweetness of unsalted butter. Some like the salty and sweet combo provided by salted butter. This butter not only works on my Sweet Cornbread but also on muffins, biscuits and toasted pound cake.

ingredients:
1 C butter, room temperature

1/4 C honey

1. In the bowl of an electric mixer, whip butter until soft and light, about 4 minutes.

2. Add the honey into mixing bowl and whip for an additional 2 minutes, making sure to scrape any butter stuck to the sides of the bowl.

3. Serve with the Sweet Cornbread, muffins, fingers, abs, etc.

Mexican Cornbread

Now that I live in Los Angeles, I have access to amazing Mexican food. But growing up, all I ever knew about Mexican cuisine I learned from Del Taco and Taco Bell. So in my mind, if it involved corn chiles or bell pepper, it was Mexican. This Mexican Cornbread may be about as authentic as the fast food joints of my childhood, but the mixture of cheeses and chiles gives the cake a moist, complex flavor that is undeniably yummy.

1. Preheat oven to 350 degrees.

2. Sift flour, baking soda, baking powder and salt together. Stir in cornmeal and set aside.

3. Using an electric mixer on a medium-low speed, combine melted butter and sugar. Mix for 30 seconds, or until incorporated.

4. Mix in eggs one at a time until well blended. Wait 30 seconds between the addition of each egg.

5. Add buttermilk and mix until incorporated.

6. With mixer on a low speed, slowly add dry ingredients until well blended and relatively lump free. Note: batter will be thick.

7. Fold in jalepeños and cheese.

8. Transfer batter to cake pans that have been greased and floured, filling until cavities are about 3/4 full.

9. Bake cornbread(s) until an inserted toothpick, (or skewer for a big ol' bundt), comes out clean—about 40 minutes for a big ol' bundt.

10. Invert on a plate and serve warm. If cornbread resists, cool in pan for 15 minutes, then invert.

ingredients:

2 C flour

1 tsp baking soda

1 tsp baking powder

1 1/2 teaspoon salt

2 C yellow cornmeal

1 C unsalted butter, melted

1 C sugar

4 eggs, room temperature

2 C buttermilk

3/4 C jalapeños peppers, cored, seeded and chopped, (about 6 average peppers)*

1 C Colby-Jack cheese, shredded

*For a milder flavor, use California green chiles.

Mac n' Cheese
Baby Bundts
For baby or mini bundt pans only

The foods we crave sometimes come from strange origins. My dad always had Stouffer's Macaroni and Cheese frozen entrees in his freezer. And that particular tang is what I think of at the mention of mac n' cheese. I've recreated—and I'd like to think improved upon—that flavor with my recipe. You can serve the macaroni from a casserole dish but baking the noodles in mini or baby bundt pans offers that, "How'd you do this?" effect.

ingredients:

5 tbsp unsalted butter, cubed

2/3 C sour cream

3/4 C whole milk

3 eggs, beaten

1 C sharp cheddar cheese, shredded

1 C semi-sharp cheddar cheese, shredded

1 C shredded colby cheese

1 tsp salt

5 C cooked elbow macaroni, drained

1. Preheat oven to 350 degrees.

2. Spray mini or baby bundt pans with a nonstick oil spray (without flour).

3. In a large saucepan over medium heat, melt butter.

4. Whisk in sour cream and milk.

5. Whisk in the beaten eggs, and continue whisking for 2 minutes.

6. Add cheeses. Continue whisking until cheese is melted and a cheese sauce is formed.

7. Season with salt.

8. With a wooden spoon, stir in the macaroni.

9. Stir 2 minutes, until cheese sauce has coated the macaroni.

10. Fill each bundt cavity to the top.

11. Bake mini bundts for 15 minutes, babies for 20 minutes.

12. Remove pans from the oven. Rest pans for 5 minutes before inverting—this lets the cheese cool and helps solidify the shape.

13. Invert pans onto a cooling rack. If the bundts won't budge from the pan, rest another 2 minutes. If, when you flip the pans, the macaroni falls out of the pan and is loose, put it back in the pan for another 2 minutes. If the bundts stick, trace the edges of the pan with a buttered knife.

Serve warm as is, with a pinch of fleur de sel on top of the bundts or garnished with steamed broccoli. *Yields approx 20 mini or 9 baby bundts*

• 8 •
Frostings

Frostings and glazes should compliment, not mask, a cake. This might seem like an obvious statement but I've seen a few too many "frosting fantasies." What I used to see only from young children frosting their first masterpiece, cloud-like puffs of frosting nearly entirely hiding any evidence of cake, seems to have become a frightening trend. I didn't really acknowledge it until the bakery received a review a few months after we opened. The critic wrote that Kiss My Bundt's cake "is the kind of cake you get if you like cake." I take that as a compliment but she didn't mean it as one. She was slighted that the cake wasn't positively bathed in frosting. Yes, I'm judging. If you can't taste the hard work that went into your cake because the frosting is that thick, what you've put on top has negated—if not ruined—what's on the bottom. (I should add that all of the recipes in this chapter create at least 2 1/2 cups of frosting per cake. At Kiss My Bundt, we're not stingy with the frosting, I believe we're *balanced.*)

Now, I will say that our frostings do have less sugar than that of many popular bakeries. Instead of making the cake sweeter, I try to use frosting to accent the flavor of the cake. For some of the cake recipes, I also recommend glazes. Glazes make a simple, sweet way to give a cake just a little extra something. I particularly love the look of a bundt with glaze accenting its ridges and curves. (For anyone trying to have their cake and eat it too, glazes make a great way to top a cake without adding extra fat.) Sometimes I use a glaze (or frosting for that matter) that offers a similar flavor to the cake in order to intensify the taste. For example, the cinnamon spice glaze makes the cinnamon pecan coffee cake out-of-this-world good.

At my shop, we frost every cake to order so that customers can pick their own flavor combination. We do give recommendations like Oreo Buttercream on Chocolate Cake. But sometimes they make their own crazy combinations, like Strawberry Cake with Oreo Buttercream (true story). While I make recommendations throughout the book for both frostings and decorations, these are based on my personal tastes and/or classic combinations. I hope that eventually you will find the confidence to experiment with any flavor you find delicious.

Decorating Your Cake

You can decorate a bundt in any number of ways. I think the shape of the bundt is beautiful and I don't believe in tarting it all up with flowers and all the other bells and whistles. But I do like to add little decorations atop the frosting that will whet your appetite for the flavors to come. (For example, I top Oreo Buttercream with an Oreo wedge and Banana Buttercream with a dried banana chip.)

Classic Kiss My Bundt toppings include:

dried fruits (including pineapple, banana, apricot and cherries)

fresh berries and citrus fruit slices (for example, a mandarin orange segment is particularly stunning atop Orange Buttercream)

wedges of cut Oreo cookies

lemon, orange and lime gummy fruit slices

colored decorators' or sanding sugar (used in coordinating colors with the cake flavor like pink on Strawberry Cake or gold on Champagne Cake)*

chocolate or other colored Jimmies

chocolate curls, chocolate shavings or mini chocolate chips (I use white, milk and dark chocolate for a more adult, gourmet version of Jimmies)*

slices or wedges of classic candies like Reese's Peanut Butter Cups and Andes' Candies (I use these when the occasion calls for seriously decadent, serious comfort food)

coffee beans and chocolate-covered coffee beans (used to add depth to the coffee flavor of the Mocha and Cappuccino Cakes)*

*See page 150 for recommended sources.

Frosting Your Cake

With the mini and baby bundts, I like to frost the top like a cupcake, not spread the frosting down the sides. To do this, I use a plastic pastry bag with a decorator tip to pipe frosting onto the cakes in a scalloped or classic twist. If you have a pastry bag, snip a bottom corner of a zip lock sandwich back and insert your decorator tip (I typically use a star tip), then add your frosting and zip the bag shut.

For a big ol' bundt, I frost the cake all the way around, including the hole. (But we leave about an inch of exposed cake at the bottom, so all the guests can see the flavor. It's that little bit of cake peeking out that really makes mouths water). If you find yourself getting crumbs in the frosting, do a thin, first coat, called the "crumb coat." Refrigerate the crumb coated cake 20 minutes to harden this layer of frosting, then apply a second coat of buttercream to cover the crumbs.

Vanilla Buttercream

Like my Basic Vanilla Birthday Cake, this frosting is my "blank canvas." Many of my variations are listed below but once you get the hang of building buttercream flavors, I encourage you to invent your own.

ingredients:

3/4 C unsalted butter, softened

3 C powdered sugar, sifted

1 tsp vanilla extract

2 tsp–2 1/2 tbsp milk, (just enough to thin buttercream to spreading consistency)

1. With an electric mixer, cream butter on medium speed.

2. Turn mixer speed to low, then slowly add powdered sugar.

3. When sugar is fully incorporated, add vanilla extract.

4. Then add your milk starting with 2 tsp and using up to 2 1/2 tbsp to thin frosting to a spreading consistency. Mix on a medium speed until frosting is smooth and fluffy.

Chocolate Buttercream

This buttercream calls for cocoa rather than melted chocolate because I love the intensity cocoa brings to the sweet frosting. I particularly like spreading it on coconut cake, then topping the whole thing with slivered almonds.

additional ingredient:

1/4 C high-fat cocoa powder, sifted*

reduce vanilla to 3/4 tsp

*See page 148 for recommended brands and sources.

Follow the instructions for Vanilla Buttercream but in step #2, add cocoa powder with the powdered sugar.

Mocha Buttercream

Follow the instructions for Vanilla Buttercream but in step #2, add cocoa powder with the powdered sugar. In step #3, add coffee extract along with the vanilla.

additional ingredients:
1/4 C high-fat cocoa powder, sifted
2 tsp coffee extract
reduce vanilla to 3/4 tsp

Irish Cream Buttercream

This variation on my Vanilla Buttercream illustrates how truly simple it is to start developing new frosting flavors.

Follow the instructions for Vanilla Buttercream but in step #4, use Irish Cream in place of milk.

additional ingredient:
2 tsp-2 1/2 tsp Irish Cream, such as Baileys

Oreo Buttercream

This frosting is my serendipitous topping. One day I took a quick break from the bakery to buy some Oreo ice cream from the shop across the street. Inhaling the aroma of baking chocolate cake while licking my ice cream, I hit upon this frosting flavor—one of the most popular items in the bakery.

ingredients:

5 Oreo cookies, (or other chocolate sandwich cookies)

3/4 C unsalted butter, softened

3 C powdered sugar, sifted

3/4 tsp vanilla extract

1–3 tbsp milk, (just enough to thin buttercream to spreading consistency)

1. In a food processor, grind Oreo cookies to a fine dust.

2. With an electric mixer, cream butter on medium speed.

3. Turn mixer speed to low, then slowly add powdered sugar.

4. When sugar is fully incorporated, add vanilla extract.

5. Then add your milk starting with 1 tbsp and using up to 3 tbsp to thin frosting to a spreading consistency. Mix on a medium speed until frosting is smooth and fluffy.

6. Fold in Oreo cookie dust.

Coconut Buttercream

ingredients:

3/4 C unsalted butter, softened

3 C powdered sugar, sifted

1 1/2 tsp coconut extract*

2 tsp- 2 1/2 tbsp milk, (just enough to thin buttercream to spreading consistency)*

*For a more subtle coconut flavor, omit the coconut extract and use coconut milk instead of cow's milk to thin the frosting.

1. With an electric mixer, cream butter on medium speed.

2. Turn mixer speed to low, then slowly add powdered sugar.

3. Add coconut extract.*

4. Then add your milk, 2 tsp at a time, using up to 2 1/2 tbsp, to thin frosting to a spreading consistency. Mix on a medium speed until frosting is smooth and fluffy.

Lemon Buttercream

1. With an electric mixer, cream butter on medium speed.
2. Turn mixer speed to low, then slowly add powdered sugar.
3. When sugar is fully incorporated, add lemon zest and extract.*
4. Then add your milk, starting with 2 tsp and using up to 2 1/2 tbsp to thin frosting to a spreading consistency. Mix on a medium speed until frosting is smooth and fluffy.

ingredients:

3/4 C unsalted butter, softened

3 C powdered sugar, sifted

zest of 1 lemon

1 tsp lemon extract, (optional)*

2 tsp-2 1/2 tbsp milk, (just enough to thin buttercream to spreading consistency)

touch of extract.

Orange Buttercream

Follow directions for Lemonade Buttercream but in step #3, swap out the lemon zest and (optional) extract for orange zest and extract.

additional ingredients:

1 1/2 tsp orange zest, (approx. the zest of 1/2 medium orange)

3/4 tsp orange extract, (optional)

Lime Buttercream

Follow directions for Lemonade Buttercream but in step #3, swap out the lemon zest and (optional) extract for lime zest and oil.

additional ingredients:

1 1/2 tsp lime zest, (approx. the zest of 1- 1 1/2 medium lime)

3/4 tsp lime oil, (optional)

Citrus Buttercream

additional ingredients:

1 1/2 tsp lime zest,
(approx. the zest of 1-
1 1/2 medium lime)

1 1/2 tsp lemon zest,
(approx. the zest of 1
small lemon)

1 1/2 tsp orange zest,
(approx. the zest of
1/2 medium orange)

Follow directions for Lemonade Buttercream but in step #3, add the orange and lime zest with the lemon zest and omit the lemon extract.

Margarita Buttercream

This buttercream was created to pair with the Margarita Cake. My favorite part about the cake is—no, not the tequila—decorating it to look like a Margarita. Roll the edges of the frosting in white decorating sugar, then garnish with a gummy lime wedge or lime zest on top. When made in mini bundt size, it is the cutest bundt ever!

ingredients:

3/4 C unsalted butter,
softened

3 C powdered sugar

1 tsp vanilla extract

3/4 tsp orange extract,
(optional)

3/4 tsp lime zest

2 1/4 tsp tequila,
(optional)

1 tsp-1 1/2 tbsp Margarita
mix, (just enough to
thin buttercream to
spreading consistency)

1. With an electric mixer, cream butter on medium speed.

2. Turn mixer speed to low, then slowly add powdered sugar.

3. When sugar is fully incorporated, add vanilla and (optional) orange extract, lime zest and (optional) tequila.

4. Then add your Margarita mix starting with 1 tsp and using up to 1 1/2 tbsp to thin frosting to a spreading consistency. Mix on a medium speed until frosting is smooth and fluffy.

Champagne Buttercream

1. With an electric mixer, cream butter on medium speed.
2. Turn mixer speed to low, then slowly add powdered sugar.
3. When sugar is fully incorporated, add vanilla.
4. Then add your Champagne Syrup starting with 1 tsp and using up to 1 1/2 tsp to thin frosting to a spreading consistency. Mix on a medium speed until frosting is smooth and fluffy.

ingredients:

3/4 C unsalted butter, softened

3 C powdered sugar, sifted

1/4 tsp vanilla extract

2 tsp-2 1/2 tbsp Champagne Syrup, (see recipe page 59)

Eggnog Buttercream

1. With an electric mixer, cream butter on medium speed.
2. Turn mixer speed to low, then slowly add powdered sugar.
3. When sugar is fully incorporated, add vanilla extract.
4. Then add your eggnog starting with 2 tsp and using up to 2 1/2 tbsp to thin frosting to a spreading consistency. Mix on a medium speed until frosting is smooth and fluffy.
5. Fold in nutmeg.

ingredients:

3/4 C unsalted butter, softened

3 C powdered sugar, sifted

1 tsp vanilla extract

2 tsp-2 1/2 tbsp eggnog, (enough to thin buttercream to a spreading consistency)

1 generous pinch nutmeg

Banana Buttercream

ingredients:

3/4 C unsalted butter, softened

3 C powdered sugar, sifted

1 tsp vanilla extract

3 tbsp banana, mashed with a fork, potato masher or hands

2 tsp- 2 tbsp milk, (enough to thin buttercream to a spreading consistency)

1. With an electric mixer, cream butter on medium speed.

2. Turn mixer speed to low, then slowly add powdered sugar.

3. When sugar is fully incorporated, add vanilla extract and banana.

4. Then add your milk starting with 2 tsp and using up to 2 tbsp to thin frosting to a spreading consistency. Mix on a medium speed until frosting is smooth and fluffy.

Straw-Raz Buttercream

My bakery manager, Megan, invented this frosting for Valentine's Day out of leftover Raspberry Purée and Strawberry Smash. It is the perfect shade of pink for the romance holiday and is absolutely delicious on vanilla, chocolate or strawberry cake.

1. With an electric mixer, cream butter on medium speed.

2. Turn mixer speed to low, then slowly add powdered sugar.

3. When sugar is fully incorporated, add vanilla extract.

4. Slowly add Raspberry Purée and Strawberry Smash. Mix on a medium speed until frosting is smooth and fluffy.*

*If mixture if thick, incrementally add 1/2 tsp of Raspberry Purée until buttercream is a spreading consistency.

ingredients:

3/4 C unsalted butter, softened

3 C powdered sugar, sifted

1 tsp vanilla extract

1 tbsp Raspberry Purée, (see recipe page 43)

1 tbsp Strawberry Smash, (see recipe page 40)

Vegan Vanilla Buttercream

I feel like a bit of a snake oil salesman calling this one buttercream since it contains neither butter nor cream! I think it is a very satisfying vegan variation on a classic, however, I find that most vegan sugars lend a slightly chalky flavor to the frosting. This can be masked by pure vanilla extract or you can try making a coconut or orange variation to help bring the flavors together.

ingredients:

3/4 C margarine

3 C vegan powdered sugar, sifted

3/4 tsp vanilla extract

2 tsp-2 1/2 tbsp soymilk, (just enough to thin buttercream to a spreading consistency)

1. With an electric mixer, cream margarine on medium speed.

2. Turn mixer speed to low, then slowly add vegan powdered sugar.

3. When sugar is fully incorporated, add vanilla extract.

4. Then add your soymilk, starting with 2 tsp and using up to 2 1/2 tbsp to thin frosting to a spreading consistency. Mix on a medium speed until frosting is smooth.

Vegan Chocolate Buttercream

additional ingredient:

1/4 C high-fat cocoa powder, sifted*

*See page 148 for recommended brands and sources.

Follow the instructions for Vegan Vanilla Buttercream but in step #2, add cocoa powder with the vegan powdered sugar.

Cream Cheese Frosting

Most bakers have little quirks about how they most enjoy their desserts. I love ice cold cream cheese frosting spread on a wedge of still-warm cake.

1. With an electric mixer on a medium speed, cream the butter and the cream cheese until soft and completely smooth, at least 2 minutes.
2. Turn the mixer speed to low and slowly add the powdered sugar 1/2 cup at a time, making sure to scrape down any frosting stuck to the sides of the bowl.
3. Add vanilla extract.
4. Mix on a medium speed until frosting is smooth and fluffy.

ingredients:

4 oz unsalted butter, softened

8 oz cream cheese, softened*

2 C powdered sugar, sifted

1/2 tsp vanilla extract

*To make a reduced fat frosting, use Neufchâtel cream cheese. (The frosting will have a more sour flavor, particularly tasty with fruit-flavored cakes like Piña Colada, 33 or Strawberry, 38.)

Almond Cream Cheese Frosting

Follow the recipe for Cream Cheese Frosting but in step #3, add almond extract in place of vanilla extract.

additional ingredient:
1/2 tsp almond extract

Coconut Cream Cheese Frosting

Follow the recipe for Cream Cheese Frosting but in step #3, add coconut extract in place of vanilla extract.

additional ingredient:
1/2 tsp coconut extract

kiss my bundt

Lemon or Orange
Cream Cheese Frosting

additional ingredients:
1/2 tsp lemon extract
or
1/2 tsp orange extract

Follow the recipe for Cream Cheese Frosting but in step #3, add lemon extract or orange extract in place of vanilla extract.

Rosewater
Cream Cheese Frosting

additional ingredient:
1/2 tsp rosewater

Follow the recipe for Cream Cheese Frosting but in step #3, add rosewater in addition to the vanilla extract.

Cinnamon
Cream Cheese Frosting

ingredients:

4 oz unsalted butter, softened

8 oz cream cheese, softened

2 C powdered sugar, sifted

1/2 tsp vanilla

1 tbsp cinnamon

1. With an electric mixer on a medium speed, cream the butter and the cream cheese until soft and completely smooth, at least 2 minutes.

2. Turn the mixer speed to low and slowly add the powdered sugar 1/2 cup at a time, making sure to scrape down any frosting stuck to the sides of the bowl.

3. Fold in vanilla extract and cinnamon.

4. Mix on a medium speed until frosting is smooth and fluffy.

Vegan Cream Cheese Frosting

1. With an electric mixer on a medium speed, combine margarine and vegan cream cheese substitute until just incorporated, 1 minute or less. (These ingredients won't cream like real butter and cream cheese, so simply mix until the two are just combined.)

2. Turn the mixer speed to low and slowly add the powdered sugar 1/2 cup at a time, making sure to scrape down any frosting stuck to the sides of the bowl.

3. Add vanilla. (You can swap out vanilla for another natural extract such as almond or coconut.)*

4. Mix on medium speed until frosting is smooth. Do not overmix or frosting may become runny.

*For additional flavor combinations, try adding 1 1/2 tsp lemon, lime or orange zest.

ingredients:

1/3 C margarine

6 oz vegan cream cheese substitute

2 C vegan powdered sugar, sifted

3/4 tsp vanilla extract

Glazing Your Cake

For glazing, the most important thing to remember is to glaze when the cake is completely cool. A hot cake is like a sponge that will absorb glaze like the Titanic taking on water. The easiest way to glaze a cooled cake is to take a 1/4 measuring cup or scoop and start pouring glaze down the ridges or in a zig zag pattern across the top of the cake.

Vanilla Glaze

ingredients:

3/4 tsp vanilla extract

1 1/2 C powdered sugar, sifted

2-3 tbsp milk, (just enough to thin mixture to glaze consistency)

1. In a small mixing bowl, combine vanilla and powdered sugar.

2. Using a whisk, add milk 1 tbsp at a time until powdered sugar is completely dissolved and mixture is just thin enough to pour over cooled cake.

Cinnamon Glaze

additional ingredient:

2 tsp ground cinnamon

Follow the recipe for Vanilla Glaze but in step #1, add 2 tsp cinnamon.

Almond Glaze

Follow the recipe for Vanilla Glaze but in step #1, add almond extract in place of vanilla extract.

additional ingredient:
3/4 tsp almond extract

Lemon Glaze

Citrus glazes bring this incredible, sweet-tart dimension to the citrus-flavored cakes. Although you might never think to call a cake "refreshing," I actually find this flavor very refreshing, even on a hot day.

1. Put sifted powdered sugar in a small mixing bowl.
2. Using a whisk, add lemon juice to powdered sugar 1 tbsp at a time until sugar is completely dissolved and mixture is just thin enough to pour over cake.

ingredients:
2 C powdered sugar, sifted
juice of 1-2 lemons

Lime Glaze

Follow the instructions for Lemon Glaze but in step #2, add the lime juice instead of lemon.

additional ingredient:
juice of 2-3 limes

Orange Glaze

additional ingredients:
2 tsp orange zest
juice of 1 medium orange

Follow the instructions for Lemon Glaze but in step #2, add the zest and use orange juice instead of lemon.

Bourbon Glaze

ingredients:
1 1/2 C powdered sugar, sifted
2- 4 tbsp bourbon, (just enough to thin mixture to glaze consistency)

1. Put sifted powdered sugar in a small mixing bowl.

2. Using a whisk, add bourbon to powdered sugar 1 tbsp at a time until sugar is completely dissolved and mixture is just thin enough to pour over cake.

Rum Glaze

ingredients:
1/2 C granulated sugar
1/4 C unsalted butter
2 tbsp water
2 tbsp rum

1. In a small saucepan, melt butter over low heat.

2. Stir sugar, water and rum into the butter, whisking until sugar is dissolved.

3. Bring mixture to a boil, boiling for 1 minute or until thick.

4. Pour over a cooled cake.

Dark Chocolate Glaze

This simple topping is a favorite of mine. One very cool thing about the glaze is that, if you top your cake then refrigerate, the glaze will form this lovely chocolate shell, not unlike the chocolate candy coating at ice cream shops.

1. In a small saucepan over medium-low heat, melt butter.

2. Remove pan from heat and mix chocolate into the butter, stirring until chocolate is completely melted.

3. Add corn syrup and whisk to a smooth, glaze.

4. Let the mixture sit for 1 or 2 minutes to allow glaze to thicken slightly before drizzling over cake.

ingredients:

3/4 C unsalted butter

6 oz premium dark chocolate, finely chopped or grated*

2 tbsp corn syrup

* See page 148 for recommended brands and sources.

kiss my bundt

Chocolate Ganache

Although the word "ganache" sounds terribly fancy, this recipe is incredibly simple. All it takes is equal parts chocolate and cream and a good whisking hand.

ingredients:

1/2 C heavy cream

4 oz (about 1/2 C) bitter-sweet 60%-70% chocolate chips or grated chocolate*

* See page 148 for rec-ommended brands and sources.

1. In a saucepan, whisk cream over medium-high heat.

2. Bring to a near boil (about 190 degrees if you have a thermometer). You do not want the cream to boil but it should be hot enough to melt the chocolate.

3. Remove from heat and stir in chocolate.

4. Whisk the chocolate into the cream until it has melted. If, after 3 minutes, the chocolate has not com-pletely melted into a glossy sauce, put the sauce pan in a heated double boiler back over heat and whisk on low heat until the chocolate has melted. Be sure to whisk and scrape the bottom of the saucepan to ensure the cream doesn't scald.

5. Ganache at this stage can be poured over the cake. Or it can be chilled for use in Molten Chocolate Minis (for recipe see page 84).

Chrysta's Whipped Cream

It's a little embarrassing to admit but until I was in high school, I thought that stuff that came in a can or a plastic tub was whipped cream. But once I was introduced to fresh whipped cream, I never looked back!

1. Place a metal bowl and a whisk attachment to an electric mixer (or your hand whisk) in the freezer for 10 minutes. Getting the bowl nice and cold helps the cream whip fast.

2. Pour the cream into the chilled bowl and begin whisking with your electric mixer at a high speed. (You can do this by hand using a wire whisk but it takes more time and a lot more muscle to get the cream finished.)

3. The cream will begin to foam, then start to grow in volume. About 1 minute into this stage you'll have fresh whipped cream.

ingredients
1 C heavy cream
1/2 tsp vanilla

Be sure not to overwhip. Overwhipping will cause the cream to "break" or lose all of its volume and turn back to an almost liquid state. On average, it takes about 4 minutes to whip 1 cup of cream with an electric mixer.

To sweeten whipped cream, add 2 tbsp of powdered sugar in step #2.

Resources

Baking Times

These baking times are approximate since most ovens vary. If you feel unsure of your oven temperature, check your cake frequently with a toothpick or cake tester for doneness. To check the accuracy of your oven temperature, purchase a small oven thermometer. (For more on baking times and temperature, see page 20.)

All cakes in this book should be baked on the center rack of the oven.

The Kiss My Bundt cake recipes are recommended for bundt pans but can be baked in any cake pan that suits your occasion following the baking times below:

Vanilla-Based Cakes

40-45 minutes for a 10-12 cup big ol' bundt
18-22 minutes for baby or "muffin" bundts
13-16 minutes for mini bundts or cupcakes
25-29 minutes for two 8" rounds or squares

Pound Cakes

55-65 minutes for a 10-12 cup big ol' bundt

Chocolate and Other Vegetable Oil-Based Cakes

45-50 minutes for a 10-12 cup big ol' bundt
20-23 minutes for baby or "muffin" bundts
14-17 minutes for mini bundts or cupcakes
28-32 minutes for two 8" rounds or squares

Vegan Cakes

30-35 minutes for a 10-12 cup big ol' bundt
14-17 minutes for baby or "muffin" bundts
10-13 minutes for mini bundts or cupcakes
18-22 minutes for two 8" rounds or squares

Troubleshooting

Your oven may have a "hot spot," and cook more quickly in one area of the oven interior than another. (Hot spots are often found at the back or front of the oven.) If you find your cake cooking too quickly on one side, turn the cake 180 degrees halfway through the baking process.

Dark colored bundt pans may cause the exterior of the cake to burn before the center is fully cooked. It is recommended to use light-colored pans.

Cocoa Powder &
Chocolate Brands and
Sources

Cocoa Powder

At the bakery, I use **Callebaut** or **Gerkens Holland** cocoa powder. They are both dark, reddish-brown, Dutch-processed cocoa powder with 22%-24% cocoa fat. I purchase my cocoa powder through a commercial distributor but if I'm caught in a pinch, I run to my local restaurant supply in Los Angeles called Surfas, www.surfasonline.com. If you're in the Los Angeles area, this is a wonderful resource.

A very good value cocoa powder on the market is **Hershey's Special Dark.** Although Hershey's does not report the percentage of butterfat, this Dutch Processed cocoa is sufficiently rich to satisfy any chocoholic.

Callebaut is also sold online at www.chocolate-source.com and www.amazon.com.

Hershey's Special Dark is sold in grocery stores and online at www.amazon.com.

Other brands of quality cocoa powder include:

Guittard, available at Sur La Table stores and online, www.surlatable.com and at www.guittard.com.

Scharffen Berger Natural Cocoa Powder, available at Sur La Table stores and online, www.surlatable.com and at www.scharffenberger.com.

Penzeys Spices Natural Cocoa Powder, available at Penzeys Spices stores and online at www.penzeys.com.

Valrohna, sold at www.chocolatesource.com and www.amazon.com.

Baking Chocolate

Callebaut Bittersweet (callets—their version of chocolate chips & blocks), available at www.chocolatesource.com and www.amazon.com.

Ghirardelli 60% Cacao Bittersweet Chips, available at grocery stores, www.ghirardelli.com and www.amazon.com.

Guittard Chucuri 65% Bittersweet Chocolate Bars, available at www.eguittard.com.

Trader Joe's Dark Chocolate (bars & blocks), available at Trader Joe's stores (see website for your nearest store, www.traderjoes.com).

(Other quality brands include: **Lindt; Scharffen Berger; Schokinag** and, for an organic alternative, **Green & Black's**).

Baking Supplies

Amazon.com

www.amazon.com

This is an extensive source for chef's tools, electric mixers, bundt pans, cocoa, chocolate, chocolate espresso beans, vanilla and other natural extracts, colored sugars and other decorations.

Beryl's Cake Decorating & Pastry Supplies

800.488.2749

www.beryls.com

Sells decorating tools, colored sugars and edible glitter, jimmies, chocolate curls and other unique and unusual decorations.

King Arthur Flour

800.827.6836

www.kingarthurflour.com

In addition to selling bulk flour, organic flour and sugar, the company sells high-quality chocolate chips and sprinkles, colored sugar and other decorations.

Kitchenaid

800.541.6390

www.kitchenaid.com

Manufactures a variety of sturdy, reliable and stylish stand mixers.

Kitchen Krafts

800.776.0575

www.kitchenkrafts.com

Offers chef's tools, mini and big ol' bundt pans, cake stands, vanilla and other extracts, decorating tools, sprinkles.

Nordic Ware

877.466.7342

www.nordicware.com/store

Creator of the bundt pan it is, of course, an excellent source for pans in every size.

Trader Joe's

(see website or phone book for your nearest store)

www.traderjoes.com

This is a terrific, inexpensive source for fresh, dried and frozen fruits, almond meal, nuts, chocolate, wine and spirits.

Sugarcraft

(internet orders only)

www.sugarcraft.com

Online retailer offering mini and baby bundt pans, cake stands, themed jimmies and sprinkles, colored sugars and edible glitter.

Surfas

866.799.4770

www.surfasonline.com

This Los Angeles-based restaurant supply carries chef's tools, mini and baby bundt pans, cocoa, bulk chocolate, vanilla and other extracts, decorating tools, jimmies and chocolate curls

Sur La Table

800.243.0852

www.surlatable.com

This home baker's dream is a one-stop shop for chef's tools, stand mixers, mini and baby bundt pans, cake stands, cocoa, vanilla and other extracts, decorating tools, colored sugars.

Whole Foods

(see website or phone book for your nearest store)
www.wholefoodsmarket.com

The gourmet grocery is a good source for vegan sugar, organic baking products, local produce, cocoa and chocolate.

Index

Acknowledgments

I'd like to thank the many people who helped me in my bundt-baking pursuits. After all, success is a group effort.

First of all, my family: Aunt Eleanor, for her motherly advice; my sisters, Jamille and Dynolis, for their support and for truly loving my bundts enough to request shipments from Los Angeles to Jacksonville and Atlanta; Uncle E.D., Uncle Johnny Lee and the rest of my family, who after tasting my bundts, have been 110% behind me, supporting me and eating my bundts clear across the country.

To Ailia, thanks for making my bakery an extension of your labor of love. And to Anagha and Anna, for being the BFFs and BGFs a girl needs during stressful and exciting times.

To those who were instrumental in making my dream of a brick and mortar bakery a reality: Erin H., Denise W., Megan K., Mary F., Kim G., Jeff V., Kelly H., Sandra G., Anagha A., and Billy and Sharon B., thank you for believing in Kiss My Bundt Bakery and putting your money where your mouth is. To Jackie J., Steve G. and Ricardo T., for helping me lay a foundation for building my bundt empire. To the 2004-2008 LAULYP Board, for helping me build friendships and relationships essential to growing my customer base in the early days.

To my FCBC family, for showing me that He has multiple plans for my life and that I can pursue my gifts. The first Kiss My Bundt Bakery Team, Megan, Jennifer, Adri and Lilly, thanks for the sacrifices you've made to help this dream of mine come true.

To the home bakers who were willing to fire up their ovens in the dead of summer to help us test all the recipes in this book.

To Margeaux Bestard, thank you for your beautiful photographs. Thanks Deborah Daly for your great artistic vision in bringing together all of the elements of this book.

To Adam, thank you for being my best friend and biggest supporter during the first year of Kiss My Bundt Bakery on 3rd Street. You helped to carry me through hard times. Your friendship and ideas (like using bacon grease) will never be forgotten.

And to Amy R., thanks for being one of the wonderful locals to embrace my bakery. You've placed a great deal of faith (and resources) in my little bundt bakeshop and somewhere along the way you became a Bundt Babe in your own right.

About
Kiss My Bundt Bakery

Kiss My Bundt is an award-winning, made-from-scratch bakery in Los Angeles specializing in bundt cakes and other Southern-inspired confections. Founded in 2005 as a web-based cake-catering company, Kiss My Bundt Bakery opened its brick-and-mortar storefront in August 2008. In its first year, the cake shop received countless accolades as one of the best bakeries in Southern California. In 2009, Kiss My Bundt began a bundt lover movement with The Baking Academy and its Intro to Baking class series created by bakery founder Chrysta Wilson.

About the Author

Chrysta Wilson grew up in the South where made-from-scratch desserts reigned supreme. She started her first bakeshop at the age of seven using her Easy Bake oven—bundt cake came later. Before returning to her first occupation, Chrysta earned a Bachelors Degree in Public Policy and a Masters Degree in Public Administration and Management from the University of Southern California. Affectionately dubbed "The Bundt Babe," for her life-long love of bundt cake, Chrysta started Kiss My Bundt Bakery in honor of her mother and the two aunts who nurtured her entrepreneurial spirit and love of baking. At Kiss My Bundt, this Los Angeles transplant is best known for her Californian spin on the Southern dessert, lightening up traditional bundt recipes and creating cakes in modern, innovative flavors.